DIAMOND★DISHES

DIAMOND DISHES

FROM THE KITCHENS OF BASEBALL'S BIGGEST STARS

MAJOR LEAGUE BASEBALL®

JULIE LORIA

LYONS PRESS
GUILFORD, CONNECTICUT
AN IMPRINT OF GLOBE PEQUOT PRESS

© MLBPA

Lyons Press is an imprint of Globe Pequot Press.

Major League Baseball players used with permission of the Major League Baseball Players Association

Major League Baseball trademarks and copyrights are used with permission of Major League Baseball Properties, Inc.

Food photography on pp. 7, 18, 26, 32, 42, 52, 61, 69, 78, 87, 92, 103, 112, 124, 130, 138, 147, 154, 164, and 170 © 2011 Ben Fink; all player photographs by EJ Camp except pp. 169 and 173 by Alexandra Penney

Design: Vertigo Design NYC
Project editor: Gregory Hyman

Library of Congress Cataloging-in-Publication Data is available on file.

ISBN 978-0-7627-6962-9

Printed in the United States of America

10 9 8 7 6 5 4 3 2 1

In memory of my mother and father

CONTENTS

I have always had a passion for food . . . and a passion for baseball!
I cherish my mother's dog-eared recipes and my father's tattered baseball glove with equal devotion. But my writing about food and baseball began with a riddle: What do the food words *pea, jam, pickle, snowcone, cheese, mustard, can of corn, meatball, pepper,* and *rhubarb* have in common? (Answer: They are all baseball expressions). From there, I started thinking about the connections between baseball and food, beyond their shared lexicon. For instance, food and baseball have emotional associations. Everyone has a favorite food or treasured meal, and everyone who follows baseball has a favorite player or beloved team, which can ignite passionate and sometimes fiery debates. We can all remember recapping a game or a meal afterward, and the discussion almost always overflows with emotion. Whether you are watching a game with family and friends or sitting down to a good meal with family and friends—or both—it's all about sharing passions to create memories across generations.

If you've been to a baseball game lately, you may have noticed that the ballpark's culinary menu has been revamped way beyond peanuts and hot dogs. It's happening across the country. At Boston's Fenway Park, you can indulge in one of the most delicious lobster rolls outside of Maine. And AT&T Park in San Francisco serves out-of-this-world garlic fries. The New York Mets' Citi Field integrates top regional cuisine via local restaurateur and avid baseball fan Danny Meyer, who brought outposts of his culinary establishments to behind center field. Even the Food Network got in on the action at New York's Yankee Stadium, with concession stands featuring guest celebrities such as *Iron Chef*'s Masaharu Morimoto. And in Miami's new ballpark, scheduled to open in 2012, the regional tastes of South Beach, from Cuban cuisine to stone crabs, will be a showstopper. Today's baseball parks are not only about baseball—they are culinary destinations, too.

The more I thought about it, the more obvious it became that cooking and watching baseball were not all that different. In fact, baseball is a lot like a great recipe. It combines skillful preparation with a mixture of exceptional ingredients and proper instruction to produce a memorable outcome. And both are social activities often enjoyed with loved ones. Some fervent fans even have a game on television while cooking dinner—or throughout the entire meal. And in the end, the experience of cooking a magical meal or watching an exciting baseball game can remain with us for years.

When it comes to the world of cooking, what could be more entertaining for baseball fans than to learn about food, family traditions, and nutritional habits from inside a

Major League Baseball player's kitchen? We live in a world where baseball players are viewed as superhuman. On the baseball diamond, these players are often idols to young and old alike, but once out of uniform, baseball players are just regular guys. Like many of us, they enjoy a good meal with family and friends. And that's what I hope *Diamond Dishes* conveys—baseball stars as regular guys.

During the last two years, I was able to interview some of the top players in the game today. And I am more than thankful to them (and their families) for letting me into their kitchens with a photographer to capture them outside their celebrity roles. Believe me when I tell you that professional athletes are real people, too. And guess what? Quite a few of them know their way around a kitchen. Sure, some players have personal chefs, but most do not. Adrian Gonzalez, Evan Longoria, and Johan Santana have knife skills that nearly rival their baseball skills, and advancing his cooking abilities is high on Paul Konerko's to-do list upon retirement. Andre Ethier's cuisine connection includes writing a food blog while on the road with his team, not to mention that he recently started breeding his own cattle. Other notable discoveries were similarities in some of the players' eating habits: Josh Johnson and Grady Sizemore still delight in family meals they grew up eating. Comfort food and carbo-loading meals like lasagna and chicken Parmesan are perpetual favorites among the players, including Roy Halladay, Joe Mauer, David Wright, and Derek Jeter. And speaking of comfort food, Lance Berkman reveals his secrets for frying catfish, while Josh Hamilton's kitchen is often filled with the aromas of his wife's home cooking. Other players, including Alex Rodriguez, Chase Utley, Ryan Howard, and Dustin Pedroia, have opted for more disciplined individual eating habits and readily discuss the benefits of organic food and green tea. Albert Pujols, Miguel Cabrera, and Hanley Ramirez, not surprisingly, all know more than a little about Latin cuisine. Making their childhood favorites, such as empanadas, arepas, and tostones, never tasted so good!

Never could I have imagined such down-to-earth conversations about food and cooking with some of baseball's biggest stars, nor the exclusive behind-the-scenes peeks into their kitchens. As a result of my culinary journey, I gathered more than sixty easy-to-make recipes derived from my conversations with each player about his favorite foods. Along the way, I discovered the dishes they love, some of their own culinary concoctions, and even a few superstitions. In this book, in addition to exploring many diamond dishes and recipes, I hope you will experience firsthand the baseball sights, sounds, and cultural tastes that penetrate our hearts, souls, and stomachs.

Bon appétit! And play ball!

"I think you feel an obligation to the fans and an obligation to your team-mates and an obligation to the organization to put your best effort out there on a daily basis and to work as hard as you can and do as well as you can because that is expected of us. It's our job."

LANCE BERKMAN

OUTFIELDER ST. LOUIS CARDINALS

★ Lance Berkman, a veteran switch-hitter with power, has been in Major League Baseball for more than ten years. When Berkman was a kid, his father noticed his ambidextrous abilities. "I am a natural left-handed thrower and a right-handed hitter," says Berkman. "But back then, right-handed hitters were kind of a dime a dozen . . . so my dad turned me around and started me hitting left-handed ever since I could swing a bat, and I've been doing it ever since. I was fortunately ambidextrous enough to be able to do it and now I feel a lot more comfortable left-handed than right-handed."

Berkman, who grew up in Texas, had spent his entire professional baseball career in his home state until the 2010 trading deadline, when he was traded midseason to the New York Yankees. He then started the 2011 season as a St. Louis Cardinal. But for the most part, fans will always equate Berkman with the Lone Star State. In the summer of 1999, the Houston Astros—not far from Berkman's hometown—selected him as a first-round draft pick. Berkman's hard work culminated in an exceptional eleven-year run with the 'Stros.

Berkman, or "The Big Puma," as Texas local talk radio designated him, recalls the witty banter that led to his nickname: "I was messing around with some guys who do a radio show in Houston. They were asking me if I ever had a nickname, and I said 'Not really.' So they said, 'If you had to give yourself a nickname, what would it be?' I said, 'Big Puma' and they asked, 'Well, why is that?' I said, 'Because I am sleek and fast and powerful,' and they thought it was hilarious and they started to call me Big Puma on the radio and it stuck."

"I'm not a huge fish eater, but I love fried catfish. I've eaten ten to twelve catfish in one sitting."

The outstanding first baseman and five-time All-Star is extraordinarily personable and exudes Southern hospitality. While holding a runner on first base, Berkman is known to shoot the breeze, but he manages to do so without breaking anyone's concentration. He says, "I talk to everybody regardless of the situation—just small talk mainly. A lot of it depends on how well I know a guy, too. Some guys I know really well and other guys I don't know as well, and with those guys the conversation is more just, 'It's hot out here, how are you swinging it, how are you feeling?' That kind of thing."

Off the field, Berkman is all Texan. "I like to hunt and fish and ranch," he says. "I've got a ranch just outside of Austin. We've got a bit of everything out there. I had a couple back-to-back horse wrecks—just bruised—so I shut that down until after my baseball career."

Berkman grew up with two younger sisters and now has four daughters. He says, with a smile, "I'm inundated with females." But he is also quick to say that, though "It would be nice to have a son . . . I wouldn't trade my girls for anything in the world."

Berkman, a devout Christian who does not drink or curse, credits his faith for keeping him grounded. He says, "Influencing others and loving others, caring for others, is what I hope that I am remembered for more than anything. That's certainly what I want my daughters to learn about." And family fun is filled with Texan traditions. He says proudly, "I just love taking them [my daughters] with me to do all my rat-killing out at the ranch. 'Rat-killing' is a catch-all term for chores—all the stuff we do out there, checking feeders or checking on the cattle or taking them fishing. I love having them with me."

These days, when it comes to home cooking, Berkman enjoys some good old Texan fare, including his favorite meal, fried catfish. "In Texas, catfish are in every river and lake. I'm not a huge fish eater, but I love fried catfish. I've eaten ten to twelve catfish in one sitting." Berkman's mother fried catfish for him as a kid, but it was his grandfather who really taught him the art of catfish frying. "My grandfather even made his own stove out of an oil drum," he adds. Berkman has a few other culinary talents when he is not playing baseball: "I've cooked quail and dove breast—wrapped in bacon with a jalapeño in the middle," he reveals. "That is pretty standard in Texas—I think everybody in the state of Texas who has ever gone quail hunting or dove hunting knows how to cook quail and dove breast." For a snack at home before a game, Berkman indulges in a simple peanut butter sandwich topped by a few added ingredients. "One thing I will eat fairly consistently before a game—because you don't want to eat too much before a game—is a peanut butter and banana sandwich with a little honey on it. I like white bread, but sometimes I feel guilty and eat wheat," he confesses. And coffee is a must for Berkman, too. "I drink a ton of coffee. I drink it every day—the stronger the better. It cannot be too strong for me. I can't drink weak coffee. I'll take matters into my own hands and make it stronger," he says.

Berkman's wife, Cara, attempts to take the matter of healthier eating into her own hands for her husband and daughters. "My wife is a real healthy eater. She's good at steaming fish or broiling fish in the oven, but I am not crazy about it," admits Berkman. Instead, Berkman prefers her organic beef tenderloin served with asparagus and a baked potato.

In the off-season, Berkman is a college football fan and roots, naturally, for the Texas teams. While watching football, pizza is what Berkman craves most: "I like the Canadian bacon and pineapple Hawaiian pizza." A unique and fun combination, just like Berkman.

FRIED CATFISH WITH SPECIAL SAUCE

MAKES 4 SERVINGS

★ For Lance Berkman, pan-fried catfish is the ideal comfort food. Years of watching his grandfather and mother fry up batches of catfishs means Berkman is at ease in the kitchen when it comes to making his own. The Berkman clan cooks catfish by coating the fish in a seasoned mixture of flour and cornmeal and then frying in plenty of oil until crispy. Do not skimp on the oil, as only deep-frying will give these fillets their golden brown crust. Berkman also shares his inside tip for knowing when the catfish are fully cooked: "They're done when they're floating." To make this simple dish even tastier, serve it with his family's favorite easy-to-make sauce.

Sauce

½ cup cocktail sauce

¼ cup tartar sauce

Catfish

4 large egg yolks

1 cup all-purpose flour

½ cup yellow cornmeal

1 teaspoon salt

½ teaspoon freshly ground black pepper

4 6-ounce skinless catfish fillets

Peanut or vegetable oil, for deep-frying

Lemon wedges, for serving

1 To make the sauce, mix the cocktail sauce and tartar sauce together in a small bowl. Set aside.

2 Beat the yolks in a shallow dish. Mix the flour, cornmeal, salt, and pepper in a second dish. Place a wax-paper-lined baking sheet near the flour and egg yolk dishes. One at a time, dip the catfish fillets in the yolks to coat, letting the excess drip back into the dish. Then dip the catfish in the flour mixture to coat, shaking off the excess. Transfer the fillets to the baking sheet. Let stand for 15 minutes to set the coating.

3 Line another baking sheet with paper towels and place it near the stove. Pour oil into a large, heavy skillet to come about one-third of the way up the side and heat over high heat until the oil shimmers on the surface. Add the catfish. (The oil should bubble immediately when you add the fish; if it doesn't, heat the oil for a few more minutes.) Fry the catfish, turning them occasionally, until golden brown and floating on the oil surface, 4–5 minutes. Using a slotted spatula, transfer the catfish to the paper towels to drain briefly.

4 Serve the catfish hot, with the lemon wedges and sauce.

HAWAIIAN PIZZA

MAKES 2–4 SERVINGS

★ In the off season, it's all about pizza for Lance Berkman. But not just any old pizza—Hawaiian pizza, which has a wildly fantastic topping of Canadian bacon and pineapple. This version gets a lift from green pepper in the sauce, and a quick roast in the oven keeps the pineapple from making the pizza soggy. You'll need a 12-inch-diameter pizza pan.

Pizza Sauce

1 tablespoon olive oil

1 small yellow onion, finely chopped

½ cup (½-inch dice) seeded green bell pepper

1 7-ounce can tomato sauce

½ teaspoon dried oregano

Pinch of crushed red pepper flakes

Pizza

2 8-ounce cans pineapple chunks in juice, drained well, patted dry with paper towels, and coarsely chopped

1 pound bag pizza dough, fresh or thawed frozen

8 ounces (2 cups) shredded mozzarella

3 ounces sliced Canadian bacon, coarsely chopped

1 To make the sauce, heat the oil in a small saucepan over medium heat. Add the onion and green pepper and cook, stirring often, until the onion is golden, about 5 minutes. Add the tomato sauce, oregano, and red pepper flakes and bring to a simmer. Reduce the heat to medium-low and simmer until the sauce is slightly reduced, about 5 minutes. Remove from the heat and allow to cool completely.

2 Position a rack in the center of the oven and preheat the oven to 425ºF.

3 Spread the pineapple on a rimmed baking sheet. Roast until excess moisture has evaporated, about 7 minutes. Set aside and allow to cool slightly. Leave the oven on.

4 On a lightly floured work surface, roll out the pizza dough to a 13-inch-diameter round. If the dough resists rolling, cover it with a kitchen towel and let it rest for a few minutes, then try again. Transfer the round to a 12-inch pizza pan. It will retract a little when moved, so stretch it to fit the pan. Spread with the cooled pizza sauce, leaving a 1-inch border around the edges. Sprinkle with the mozzarella, the pineapple, and then the Canadian bacon.

5 Bake pizza until the crust is golden brown, 17 to 20 minutes. Let stand a few minutes, then cut into wedges and serve hot.

BEEF TENDERLOIN WITH ROASTED ASPARAGUS AND MUSHROOM-PORT SAUCE

MAKES 6–8 SERVINGS

★ Lance Berkman's wife, Cara, turns to this easy, first-class dish as her go-to main course for special occasions. The cooked beef needs to rest for at least fifteen minutes before carving, which is a perfect time to roast the asparagus spears and finish the sauce. Retained heat will continue to cook the beef during the rest period, so the beef should be removed from the oven when it is five to ten degrees below the desired internal temperature. Don't guess—use a meat thermometer! A reasonably priced Californian tawny or ruby port is perfect for making the mushroom sauce.

Mushroom-Port Sauce

2 tablespoons unsalted butter

10 ounces cremini or white mushrooms, sliced

2 tablespoons minced shallots

2 tablespoons all-purpose flour

2 cups beef broth, preferably homemade (or use canned reduced-sodium beef broth)

1/3 cup tawny or ruby port

1/2 teaspoon tomato paste

1/2 teaspoon chopped fresh thyme

Salt and freshly ground black pepper

Beef Tenderloin

1 3-pound trimmed beef tenderloin, patted dry and tied

2 garlic cloves, cut into 6 slivers

2 tablespoons vegetable oil

1½ teaspoons salt

1/2 teaspoon freshly ground black pepper

5 sprigs of fresh thyme, plus more for garnish

2 tablespoon unsalted butter, sliced

Asparagus

2 pounds asparagus, woody bottoms discarded

1 tablespoon extra-virgin olive oil

Salt and freshly ground black pepper

1 To make the sauce, melt the butter in a large skillet over medium-high heat. Add the mushrooms and cook, stirring often, until they are beginning to brown, about 7 minutes. Add the shallots and cook until softened, about 2 minutes. Sprinkle with the flour and stir well. Stir in the broth, port, tomato paste, and thyme and bring to a simmer. Reduce the heat to medium-low and simmer uncovered, stirring often, until slightly thickened, about 10 minutes. Season with salt and pepper. (The sauce can be prepared up to 1 day ahead, cooled, covered, and refrigerated.)

2 Position a rack in the center of the oven and preheat the oven to 450°F.

3 Using a small knife, make 6 incisions in the beef, spacing them evenly all around the roast. Insert a garlic sliver into each incision. Rub the beef with 1 tablespoon oil, then season with salt and pepper. Heat the remaining 1 tablespoon oil in a large oven-proof skillet or a metal roasting pan just large enough to hold the beef over medium-high heat. Add the beef and sear, turning occasionally, including the ends, until browned, about 8 minutes. Remove from the heat.

4 Add the thyme to the pan, and place the butter slices on top of the beef. Roast, without turning, until an instant-read thermometer inserted in the center

of the beef reads 125ºF for medium-rare, about 25 minutes. Transfer the beef to a carving board, and let stand at room temperature for 15 minutes. Pour the pan juices into a small glass bowl and set the bowl and the skillet aside.

5 Arrange the asparagus in a single layer in a large rimmed baking sheet (an 18 x 13-inch half sheet pan is perfect). Drizzle with the olive oil and roll in the oil to coat. Season with salt and pepper. Roast until the asparagus is barely tender, about 12 minutes, depending on the thickness of the asparagus.

6 Meanwhile, finish the sauce. Skim off and discard the fat from the surface of the pan juices. Heat the skillet over medium heat until sizzling. Add the mushroom sauce and the degreased pan juices to the skillet and heat, stirring to release the browned bits in the pan, until simmering. Turn the heat to very low, cover, and keep warm.

7 Untie the beef and carve crosswise into ½-inch-thick slices. Arrange on a platter, pour any carving juices over the meat, and garnish with additional thyme. Pour the sauce into a sauceboat. Transfer the asparagus to a warm serving platter. Serve immediately.

PEANUT BUTTER, BANANA, AND HONEY ON WHOLE WHEAT SANDWICH

MAKES 1 SERVING

★ Whether you play professional baseball or not, you can use a good midday energy boost. Berkman swears by this almost-daily quick and easy sandwich. Use your favorite peanut butter and your preferred honey, and you, too, might find yourself making this delightful afternoon treat nearly every day.

2 slices whole wheat bread

3 tablespoons peanut butter

½ banana, peeled and sliced into ¼-inch rounds

1 tablespoon of your favorite honey

Spread one slice of bread with the peanut butter. Top with overlapping banana slices, then drizzle with the honey. Add the other slice of bread, and pat the top lightly. Cut in half and serve.

> "It is like a dream coming true … baseball is more than just a game. It is my passion. It is what I love. I love everything about it."

MIGUEL CABRERA

FIRST BASEMAN DETROIT TIGERS

★ Miguel Cabrera is one of the most dangerous hitters in baseball today, a young All-Star who clearly has the game embedded in his DNA. For starters, the naturally gifted Cabrera inherited more than a few athletic genes from his mother, a fifteen-year softball player for Venezuela's national team. And Cabrera's uncle founded a Venezuelan baseball school, practically in Cabrera's backyard. "I grew up with a baseball family, and that's why I wanted to play baseball. I wanted to be good," says Cabrera.

Like loads of kids, Cabrera's childhood dream was to play professional baseball. "Since I was twelve, I knew I wanted to play professional baseball someday," he says. And Cabrera was among the tiny percentage of players whose dream actually came true. With a meteoric ascent through the Minor Leagues, it took no time at all for him to make his Major League debut, on June 20, 2003, at the young age of twenty. That day, Cabrera launched his Big League career in dramatic fashion by hitting a walk-off home run to dead center field. In the afterglow of his blockbuster first game, he gained the immediate respect of his teammates and coaches, becoming a regular fixture on the roster. He was affectionately renamed "The Kid" around the Marlins clubhouse. In the following four months, his extraordinary talent became noticeable around baseball as he helped his team capture a World Series championship. "Winning the World Series in 2003 was my highest career moment," he readily admits.

When all is said and done, Cabrera is a baseball whiz. He has played nearly every position on the field since his Major League start. He says, "All my career I moved around everywhere, right field, left field, shortstop." Today, he is the first baseman for the Detroit

"I love cheese. There is always cheese in my refrigerator."

Tigers, a five-time All-Star, and a three-time Silver Slugger recipient. But Cabrera is reflective about his natural-born ability. He says, "I think God gave me a gift to play baseball. I always think a lot about someone giving you a gift—you don't throw it away." Instead, Cabrera strives to improve every day: "I want to be one of the best players in the game and to get better and better. Whatever happens, if it is down or up, you have to stay up. And you have to try, try hard."

Best known for his big-time hitting, Cabrera has a simple warm-up routine for game day. Unlike some professional athletes, who use a specific number of bat swings as an unbreakable pregame ritual, Cabrera relies on instinct. He says, "I swing the bat to get loose. I do it until I feel good. When I feel good, I feel I am prepared for the game and can go out there and do my best." But on the rare occasion Cabrera is not crushing the ball in his usual way, he admits to making a small change in his routine: "When I'm not hitting, I will change something like my cleats, or my batting glove, that's it. Everything else I do the same." And before game time, Cabrera takes a few moments to prepare mentally, too. He says, "I put on my headphones and listen to music so I get relaxed before a game. The music makes me get more focused and gets me excited to get out there and do my hitting."

Born and raised in Maracay, a hotbed for baseball superstars, Cabrera has not lost his Venezuelan roots. When it comes to traditional hometown cuisine, Cabrera cannot live without the classic arepa. Though not a cook himself, he knows how to prepare arepas. "I think everybody from Venezuela knows how to cook arepas," he says. The tried and true cornmeal patty is filled with cheese, chicken, or steak; Cabrera's simple version is filled with a Venezuelan cheese known as Guayanés. "I love cheese," says Cabrera. "There is always cheese in my refrigerator." Whether he eats cheese by itself or as an ingredient, Cabrera admits he is a fanatic. His favorite indulgences are an occasional cheesesteak sandwich and cheesecake for dessert. But on the healthier side, Cabrera also likes a salmon fillet and a Caesar salad. He says, "In Venezuela, we have all different food where I grew up. We have rice and beans, we have chicken, fish, and we have pasta. We have a lot of Italian restaurants where I lived, so I think pasta is my favorite food, with Parmesan cheese," he adds with a smile.

In the off-season, Cabrera travels with his wife, Rosangel, and their two daughters. "We started doing this a couple of years ago—every November we try to go somewhere," he says. "Last year we went to Hawaii. And this year, we will be going to Spain." Closer to home, he enjoys bike riding with his four-year-old daughter or watching her play tennis. Without a doubt, she, too, will have a natural talent for hitting the ball hard.

CAESAR SALAD

MAKES 4 SERVINGS

★ A Caesar salad is a great way to start a meal, of course, but it also makes a leafy entree with added meat, fish, or poultry. Miguel Cabrera enjoys it as a complement to any meal. The dressing in this version is made in the blender, which gives it a creamy thickness without the raw egg of the traditional recipe.

Caesar Dressing

2 tablespoons red wine vinegar

2 tablespoons freshly grated Parmesan

1 teaspoon Dijon mustard

1 teaspoon anchovy paste or 2 anchovy fillets, drained and coarsely chopped

1 teaspoon Worcestershire sauce

1 garlic clove, peeled and crushed

²/₃ cup extra-virgin olive oil

Salad

2 romaine hearts (about 15 ounces), washed and torn into bite-size pieces

1 cup croutons

½ cup (2 ounces) freshly shredded Parmesan

Freshly ground black pepper

1 To make the dressing, process the vinegar, Parmesan, mustard, anchovy paste, Worcestershire sauce, and garlic in a blender until the garlic is pureed. With the machine running, gradually add the oil. (The dressing can be refrigerated in a jar for up to 3 days. Shake well before using.)

2 Combine the romaine and croutons in a large bowl. Add the dressing and Parmesan and toss. Add a few grinds of pepper, and toss again. Serve chilled.

CHEESESTEAK WITH PROVOLONE AND THREE-VEGETABLE TOPPING

MAKES 4 SERVINGS

★ Miguel is crazy for anything with cheese, and a hearty cheesesteak sandwich is no exception. Cheesesteaks call for thinly sliced steak, which may seem daunting at home, but the trick is to freeze the steak, which allows for precise slicing. Add sautéed onions, peppers, and mushrooms, and a topping of melted provolone cheese, and you'll have a favorite fast food homemade in your kitchen. Just be sure to have plenty of napkins nearby—it's good to the very last bite.

2 rib-eye steaks (10 ounces each)

Salt and freshly ground black pepper

2 tablespoons olive oil

1 large yellow onion, cut into ¼-inch-thick half-moons

1 medium red bell pepper, seeded and cut into ¼-inch-thick strips

8 ounces white mushrooms, sliced

6 ounces thinly sliced provolone cheese

4 crusty oblong rolls, split lengthwise

1 Freeze the steaks until semisolid and firm enough to slice thinly, about 1 hour. Using a narrow carving knife, cut the steaks across the grain as thinly as possible. Place on a plate and season with 1 teaspoon salt and ½ teaspoon pepper. Let stand at room temperature until thawed, about 30 minutes.

2 Heat 1 tablespoon oil in a large skillet over medium-high heat. Add the onion, red pepper, and mushrooms and cook, stirring occasionally, until the onions and peppers are very tender, about 12 minutes. Season with salt and pepper. Transfer to a bowl and cover with aluminum foil to keep warm.

3 Position a broiler rack about 8 inches from the heat and preheat the broiler.

4 Heat the remaining 1 tablespoon oil in a griddle or large skillet over medium-high heat. Add the steak slices and spread them out so as much meat as possible is in direct contact with the griddle. You want the steak to brown, not steam. Cook until the underside is browned, about 1 minute. Turn the steak slices and cook just until the other side is browned, about 1 minute longer. Using a wide spatula, transfer the steak slices to a bowl.

5 Divide the meat, then the provolone, evenly among the opened rolls. Place on a broiler pan. Broil just until the cheese melts, about 1 minute. Transfer each sandwich to a plate, top each with some of the vegetable mixture, and serve hot.

SHRIMP AND SAFFRON RISOTTO

MAKES 6 FIRST COURSE OR 4 MAIN COURSE SERVINGS

★ When he is not enjoying traditional Venezuelan cuisine, Miguel Cabrera loves to eat Italian food, and risotto is at the top of his list of favorites. Use starchy, medium-grain rice, such as Italian Arborio (available at supermarkets) or Carnaroli (more difficult to find, but worth the search) for risotto: Long-grain rice won't do. Almost-constant stirring releases the starch from the rice and lends the dish its famous creaminess. The added Parmesan cheese is a must, especially for Cabrera!

1 pound large shrimp

5 cups canned reduced-sodium chicken broth

2 tablespoons olive oil

1 small yellow onion, finely chopped

1 garlic clove, minced

1½ cups risotto rice, such as Arborio or Carnaroli

½ cup dry white wine, such as Pinot Grigio

2 ripe plum tomatoes, seeded and diced

½ teaspoon crushed saffron threads

½ cup freshly grated Parmesan, plus more for serving

¼ cup heavy cream

Salt and freshly ground black pepper

Chopped fresh parsley, for garnish

1 Peel and devein the shrimp, reserving the shells. Butterfly each shrimp by cutting almost completely open along the curvature where the vein was. Refrigerate the shrimp.

2 Combine the broth, 1 cup water, and the reserved shells in a medium saucepan and bring to a boil over high heat. Reduce the heat to medium-low and simmer for 10 minutes. Using a wire sieve, scoop out and discard the shells. Reduce the heat to very low so the stock stays hot.

3 Heat the oil in a large, heavy-bottomed saucepan over medium heat. Add the onion and cook until softened, about 3 minutes. Add the garlic and cook until fragrant, about 1 minute. Add the rice and cook, stirring often, until the rice looks mostly translucent, about 3 minutes. Pour in the wine and cook until reduced by half, about 1 minute.

4 Stir about ¾ cup hot stock into the rice. Cook, stirring almost constantly, until the rice absorbs almost all of the stock, about 3 minutes. Adjust the heat so the rice stays at a steady simmer. Stir in another addition of stock, and stir almost constantly until the liquid is almost absorbed. Repeat, adding more stock as it is absorbed, until you use nearly all of the stock and the rice is barely tender, 20–25 minutes. If you run out of stock and the rice isn't tender, add hot water.

5 Add the shrimp, tomatoes, and saffron and cook until the shrimp is firm and opaque, about 3 minutes. Stir in ½ cup Parmesan and the heavy cream. Add the rest of the stock to give the risotto a loose, runny consistency. Season with salt and pepper.

6 Spoon the risotto into deep bowls and sprinkle with the parsley. Serve hot, with additional Parmesan on the side.

> "You want to get your shot in the Major Leagues, but you don't just want to make it. You want to be able to stick and have fun."

ON THE MENU
MANGO AND CUCUMBER SALSA-SALAD
LAZY ENCHILADAS
OLD-FASHIONED CHERRY PIE

ANDRE ETHIER

OUTFIELDER LOS ANGELES DODGERS

★ Andre Ethier has an action-packed life in his pivotal role as an outfielder for the Los Angeles Dodgers. Since making his Major League debut for the Dodgers on May 2, 2006, Ethier has continued to excel, putting up big numbers and successfully wearing out pitchers along the way. And Ethier is no stranger to persistence. As the oldest of three boys, he displayed an ingrained enthusiasm for baseball that exhausted his brothers and father. He recalls, "From what my parents told me, I had a different drive. For instance, we'd go to the park and practice, and my other brothers would be satisfied after a little bit of swinging and think they had done enough, but I was always the one saying, 'One more, one more, one more, let's try one more, let's do this one more time.'" And the determined young Ethier would not let up. He says, "After a while, my other brothers would be sitting over on the bench or doing something else and I would be dragging my dad back out for one more pop fly, or to toss me one more ball. I think it was that stubbornness and that pursuit of perfection that kept me going."

In the last few years, Ethier has transformed himself into one of baseball's top outfielders. Through hard work and relentless effort, he has achieved a Silver Slugger Award and a spot on the 2010 National League All-Star team. And his momentum keeps building. "Since my call-up in '06, I feel that each year I have gotten better, become a better baseball player statistically, and become a better teammate," he says.

Ethier and his wife, Maggie, divide their time between Los Angeles during the regular season and Phoenix in the winter months and during Spring Training. When not caught up in the action on the diamond, Ethier is exploring his passion for food. A few years ago,

"I can't turn down cherry pie . . . When I see that ceramic dish on the counter, I know there is a cherry pie underneath it."

he launched a food blog to coincide with the Dodgers' relocation of their Spring Training facility to Phoenix, where Ethier was born and raised. During his Spring Training road trips, Ethier would keep copious notes on the restaurants he visited. "I wanted to write an experience from a personal perspective," he recalls. "I never wrote from the point of view where I was too critical. There were restaurants that I enjoyed and I thought were good, and I wanted it to be positive." Over time, however, his blogging took a backseat to his escalating baseball career and his active family life. "I had the time to do it at first, but the off-the-field stuff has become more demanding," he says. "Now, I don't have much time to sit at home and write with my young son wanting to play." But when the time is right, Ethier may revisit this idea again, one way or another.

Currently, Ethier is focusing on a new food interest. "Right now I am getting into breeding my own cattle to produce my own beef. I just got an Angus cow and I'm going to start breeding it, and at least know what I am feeding it. I can't be too hands-on during the season, so my wife's parents help out. We are doing the chicken thing with egg producing, too. We are trying to be more self-reliant."

During the off-season, being more self-reliant also means enjoying more home-cooked meals with Maggie and his young sons, especially after seven months on the road. When it comes to meals, Ethier sticks to what he knows best. He says, "I don't do any cooking. I do the eating. I think that's why I became good at knowing restaurants because I don't do much cooking myself. My wife does all the stuff. She does everything." A few of Ethier's favorite meals include his wife's enchiladas, chicken quesadillas, and a chopped mango salsa that even he admits to knowing how to make. He says, "My mother and my grandmother made it. In L.A. there are fresh food stands that make it. It's a good thing to eat in the summer." He also loves the Middle Eastern eateries in L.A.: "My favorite thing I eat almost every day is a club chicken schnitzel pita with extra hummus."

But when it comes to dessert, Ethier has just one favorite. "I can't turn down cherry pie," he admits. Although Ethier's cherry pie intake is usually limited to once or maybe twice a month, everyone in his family knows how much he loves it. His wife learned to make his favorite dessert, and his grandmother bought him his very own ceramic pie dish for safekeeping a freshly made pie. Says Ethier proudly, "When I see that ceramic dish on the counter, I know there is a cherry pie underneath it."

MANGO AND CUCUMBER SALSA-SALAD

MAKES 2 CUPS

★ This refreshing combination of sweet and spicy is Andre's specialty (he says it is the only thing he really makes in the kitchen), and he makes it often, usually as a salad on a hot summer day during baseball season. But it also makes a fine salsa to dress up simply grilled salmon or tuna. The salsa-salad is especially refreshing served chilled.

2 large ripe mangos
1 medium cucumber
3 tablespoons freshly squeezed lime juice
1 teaspoon hot red pepper sauce
Salt

1 Place a mango on the work surface. The pit, which is about ½ inch thick, runs horizontally through the center of the fruit. Use a sharp knife to cut off the top of the fruit, slicing just above the top of the pit. Turn the mango over and cut off the other side of the fruit. Using a large metal spoon, scoop the mango flesh from each portion in one piece. Cut the mango flesh into ½-inch dice. If you wish, cut the mango flesh from the pit, too. Repeat with the second mango. Transfer dice to a bowl.

2 Peel the cucumber. Cut it in half lengthwise, and use the tip of a teaspoon to scoop out the seeds. Cut the cucumber into ½-inch dice and add to the bowl. Add the lime juice and hot pepper sauce, season with salt, and stir to combine. Cover and refrigerate until chilled, at least 1 hour and up to 8 hours. Serve chilled.

LAZY ENCHILADAS

MAKES 8 SERVINGS

★ This recipe for a Tex-Mex casserole is in the collections of many good cooks, including Andre Ethier's wife, Maggie. It relies heavily on convenience foods, but it has from-scratch flavor. If you want to be especially lazy, use 4 cups coarsely chopped chicken pulled from a rotisserie bird.

1 tablespoon vegetable oil

3 8-ounce boneless and skinless chicken breast halves

½ teaspoon salt

¼ teaspoon freshly ground black pepper

Cooking oil spray, for the baking dish and tortillas

18 7-inch corn tortillas, cut into sixths

1 16-ounce container sour cream

1 16-ounce jar green salsa

1 10¾-ounce can cream of chicken soup

2 4½-ounce cans chopped mild green chiles, drained and rinsed

1 8-ounce package Mexican-blend shredded cheese

1 Heat the oil in a large skillet over medium heat. Add the chicken and cook, turning once, until browned on both sides, about 6 minutes. Add enough water to barely cover and bring to a simmer. Season with salt and pepper. Reduce the heat to medium-low and cover. Simmer until cooked through, about 20 minutes. Remove the chicken from the skillet and let cool. Cut the chicken into bite-size pieces.

2 Position racks in the center and upper third of the oven and preheat to 350°F. Lightly spray a 13 x 9-inch baking dish with oil.

3 Spread the tortillas on 2 baking sheets. Spray lightly with cooking oil spray. Bake until crisp, 10 to 15 minutes. Let cool on the baking sheets.

4 Whisk the sour cream, salsa, soup, and chiles together in a large bowl. Thinly spread about ⅓ cup of the sour cream mixture in the bottom of the baking dish. Add the chopped chicken to the remaining sour cream mixture and stir to combine. Spread one-third of the tortillas in the dish, then cover with one-third of the remaining sour cream mixture. Sprinkle with one-third of the cheese. Repeat with another third of the tortillas, sour cream mixture, and cheese. Repeat again, ending with the cheese.

5 Bake in the center of the oven until casserole is bubbling and the cheese is melted, about 35 minutes. Let stand for 5 minutes, then serve hot.

OLD-FASHIONED CHERRY PIE

MAKES 8 SERVINGS

★ When it comes to choosing a dessert, Andre Ethier always picks cherry pie. This version comes from one of his favorite places, Rock Springs Café, not far from Phoenix. Cherries come in a few varieties: Sour cherries (also called tart cherries), available frozen at most supermarkets, give the pie its familiar, distinctive flavor, but you can also use fresh pitted sweet Bing cherries.

Flaky Pie Dough

2 cups all-purpose flour, plus more for rolling out the dough

1½ tablespoons sugar

½ teaspoon salt

6 tablespoons (¾ stick) cold unsalted butter, cut into ½-inch cubes

6 tablespoons vegetable shortening, chilled, cut into ½-inch cubes

⅓ cup ice water, or as needed

1 teaspoon milk

2 teaspoons sugar

Cherry Filling

5 cups frozen pitted sour (tart) cherries, unthawed (see Note)

1¼ cups sugar

3 tablespoons instant tapioca, ground into a powder in a blender or coffee grinder

2 tablespoons freshly squeezed lemon juice

¼ teaspoon salt

⅛ teaspoon almond extract

2 tablespoons unsalted butter, thinly sliced, optional

1 To make the pie dough, mix the flour, sugar, and salt together in a medium bowl. Add the butter and shortening. Using a pastry blender or two knives, cut the fats into the flour until the mixture looks like coarse crumbs with some pea-sized pieces. Using a fork, gradually stir in ice water until the mixture is evenly moistened and begins to clump together. (You may need more or less water.) Gather up the dough and cut into two portions, one slightly larger than the other. Shape each portion into a flat disk, and wrap each in plastic wrap. Refrigerate for at least 1 hour and up to 2 hours. The dough is easiest to roll out if chilled, but not hard.

2 Position a rack in the bottom third of the oven and preheat to 400°F. Line a rimmed baking sheet with aluminum foil.

3 To make the filling, combine the frozen cherries, sugar, ground tapioca, lemon juice, salt, and almond extract in a large bowl. Let stand while rolling out the dough.

4 On a lightly floured work surface, roll the larger pastry disk into a 13-inch-diameter round about ⅛ inch thick. Transfer to a 9-inch pie dish. Add the filling and scatter the butter, if using, on top. Roll out the remaining disk into a 10-inch-diameter round about ⅛ inch thick and center on top of the filling. Trim the excess dough to ½ inch beyond the edge of the dish. Pinch the top and bottom crust together and flute the edges. Place pie dish on the baking sheet. Lightly brush top crust evenly with milk. Finish by sprinkling remaining sugar across the top.

5 Bake pie for 15 minutes. Reduce the oven temperature to 350°F and continue baking until the juices are bubbling and the crust is golden brown, about 1¼ hours. Transfer to a wire cake rack and let cool completely. Slice into wedges and serve.

NOTE: Sour cherries are available fresh in the early summer at farmers' markets and at some fruit stands and produce markets. You'll need to buy about 4 pounds of sour cherries to get 5 cups of pitted cherries. Canned pitted tart cherries in juice, well drained, are also an option. If using fresh or canned cherries instead of frozen, the baking time may be slightly reduced—check for bubbling juices after 1 hour. Sweet Bing cherries are an option, but reduce the sugar to ½ cup.

> "Playing for a new team is exciting. Boston has great fans and history. The times I spent in San Diego were wonderful, and I will never forget my times as a Padre. But it is now time to look toward a new adventure."

ON THE MENU

GUACAMOLE GONZALEZ
RIB-EYE STEAK SOFT TACOS WITH GRILLED-TOMATO SALSA
CHILES RELLENOS

ADRIAN GONZALEZ

FIRST BASEMAN BOSTON RED SOX

★ During his seven full Major League seasons, Adrian Gonzalez played a key role in the San Diego lineup. Some of his career highlights include helping the Padres produce ninety wins in 2010 and playing alongside his brother during much of the 2008 and 2009 seasons. "It was pretty special to be able to play for the Padres and be able to share all the different things that I went through with my brother by being on the same team," says Gonzalez. "It was a pretty special ride." Though four years younger than Edgar, Adrian made it to the big leagues well ahead of his brother. As a veteran, he could be a mentoring teammate to his brother, who now plays in Japan. Says Gonzalez, "We always kind of both gave each other advice on different aspects of life. It was pretty neat to be able to play together for the same team and for the team we grew up wanting to play for."

At the start of his eighth season, the Pacific Coast native and three-time All Star has begun a new chapter in his career. On December 6, 2010, Gonzalez became a member of the Boston Red Sox, and he is now looking forward to playing on the East Coast. He says, "Playing for a new team is exciting. Boston has great fans and history. The times I spent in San Diego were wonderful, and I will never forget my times as a Padre. But it is now time to look toward this new adventure."

Gonzalez grew up in San Diego but spent part of his childhood in Mexico, his parents' homeland. He credits his experiences learning baseball from both the American and Mexican perspective as invaluable. He recalls, "I learned to play on both sides of the border, which is pretty awesome, but it's definitely a different style of baseball from one to the other." According to Gonzalez, the Mexican baseball experience was more casual than the

> "My mom, my wife, and my mother-in-law all make [chiles rellenos]. And I make them, too."

American approach to the game: "On the Mexican side, everything is a little more relaxed, with less emphasis on mechanics. You know, it's just go out there and play and everyone has a little more flare. The talent is pretty even for both until you get to age fifteen, and that is when you see the big jump. In Mexico a lot of young players go on to work and don't continue the pursuit of playing baseball. In the U.S. you see a lot more pursuit and dedication." He also adds, "As a fourteen year old, I got to play against top-level thirty-year-old players in Mexico. That was very good for me because I was able to learn a lot of instincts and maturity that you wouldn't see at a young age. I was able to learn a lot from both sides."

For Gonzalez, dinner after a game is often at home with friends and family and his wife, Betsy. His favorite homemade Mexican meal is stuffed poblano peppers, more commonly known as chiles rellenos. He says proudly, "My mom, my wife, and my mother-in-law all make them. And I make them, too." Gonzalez learned some of his own culinary skills as a child watching his mother cook. His specialties include scrambled eggs with pico de gallo, quesadillas, homemade guacamole, and tacos. "I could eat tacos every day," admits Gonzales. Before heading to the ballpark, Gonzales likes to eat a big meal, but not always a Mexican dish. "Sometimes I'll eat a hamburger and two slices of pizza for lunch," says the physically fit All-Star first baseman.

Gonzalez and his wife enjoy hanging out at home together. They live with their three dogs, Princess, Pepito, and Toby—a teacup poodle, teacup Chihuahua, and teacup Maltese, each weighing less than five pounds. Gonzales and his wife, Betsy, met in middle school. As teenagers, "I liked her more than she liked me," he claims. A true romantic, Gonzalez once hired a plane to fly a banner overhead with the words "I love you, Betsy." He adds with a smile, "Now she teases me about being more romantic before we were married, but I tell her I had more free time back then."

In addition to the demands of a full baseball season, Gonzalez and Betsy are devoted supporters of their church as well as of various charitable events for the community. In 2008, they founded the Adrian and Betsy Gonzalez Foundation, an organization that supports disadvantaged children in areas of education, health, and athletics. Together, they host several events, fund-raise, and "try and help out the community any way we can," says Gonzalez.

In the off-season, Gonzalez and his wife like to travel, and they recently took a first-time trip to Europe. They explored Barcelona, Madrid, Paris, Florence, and Rome. "Paris and Rome were our favorite places," says Gonzalez. And now he can add Boston to his list of favorite places to explore.

RIB-EYE STEAK SOFT TACOS WITH GRILLED-TOMATO SALSA

MAKES 4 SERVINGS

★ This family-style Mexican dish is directly from the kitchen of Adrian Gonzalez. It is at its best when the tomatoes and beef are grilled outdoors, but go ahead and broil them inside when the weather isn't cooperating (warm the tortillas in an oven or microwave according to the package directions). These tacos are all about the beef.

Grilled-Tomato Salsa

4 ripe plum tomatoes, cored

¼ cup finely chopped white onion

2 tablespoons finely chopped fresh cilantro

1 serrano chile, seeded and minced

1 tablespoon freshly squeezed lime juice

1 garlic clove, crushed through a press, optional

Salt

Tacos

½ cup finely chopped white onion

2 tablespoons finely chopped fresh cilantro

2 10-ounce boneless rib-eye steaks

1 teaspoon salt

½ teaspoon freshly ground black pepper

8 7-inch corn tortillas

Guacamole Gonzalez (page 34)

1 Prepare a hot fire in an outdoor grill.

2 To make the salsa, place the tomatoes on the grill. Cover and grill, turning occasionally, until the skins are blackened and split, about 5 minutes. Transfer to a bowl and set aside until cool enough to handle. Peel, seed, and dice the tomatoes and transfer to a bowl. Add the onion, cilantro, chile, lime juice, and garlic, if using, and season with salt. Set aside. (If you like cold salsa, place the bowl in another bowl of ice water to chill quickly.)

3 Mix the white onion and cilantro in a small bowl and set aside. Season the steaks with salt and pepper.

4 Lightly oil the grill grate. Place the steaks on the grill and cover. Grill, turning after 3 minutes, until the steaks feel somewhat firmer than raw meat, about 6 minutes for medium-rare. Transfer to a carving board and let stand for 3 minutes.

5 Meanwhile, place the tortillas on the grill, cover, and grill, turning once, until warmed through, about 1 minute. Transfer to a napkin-lined basket and wrap in the napkin to keep warm.

6 Cut the steaks across the grain into thin slices, discarding any excess fat. Transfer the sliced steak, with any carving juices, to a serving bowl. Serve the steak, with tortillas, white onion mixture, salsa, and guacamole, letting each person assemble his or her own.

GUACAMOLE GONZALEZ

MAKES ABOUT 4 CUPS

⭐ In addition to his skill as a first baseman, Adrian Gonzalez makes a crazy-good guacamole. Be sure to use ripe Hass avocados with pebbly dark skins and white onion for authentic Mexican flavor. Gonzalez isn't a garlic fan, so he leaves it out, but you can add as much as you like. Have lots of tortilla chips and a group of friends on hand, because this makes a big batch. It is also a major component of the soft tacos on page 33.

6 ripe Hass avocados
⅓ cup finely chopped white onion
1–2 serrano chiles, seeded and minced
1 medium tomato, seeded and diced
3 tablespoons finely chopped fresh cilantro
3 tablespoons freshly squeezed lime juice
1–2 garlic cloves, minced, optional
Salt and freshly ground black pepper
Tortilla chips, for serving

1   One at a time, cut the avocados in half lengthwise. Twist the two halves in opposite directions, and pull apart to reveal the pit. Dig out the pit with a spoon. Scoop the avocado flesh into a medium bowl.

2   Add the onion and chiles. Using a large fork, coarsely mash the avocados—the mixture should not be smooth. Add the tomato, cilantro, lime juice, and garlic, if using, and mix well. Season with salt and pepper (you may need more salt than you think, as the avocados can take a good amount of seasoning).

3   Transfer to a serving bowl and serve immediately, with the tortilla chips for dipping. (The guacamole can be made up and refrigerated up to 8 hours in advance, with plastic wrap pressed directly on its surface to keep out air.)

CHILES RELLENOS

MAKES 6 SERVINGS

★ Stuffed chiles are one of the glories of Mexican cuisine: just ask Adrian Gonzalez and his wife, Betsy, who shared their family recipe with me. You can use any kind of large mild chile. The Gonzalez family likes poblanos, but Anaheims, New Mexico chiles, or cubanelle peppers are good, too. As an alternative to the more commonly used Monterey Jack or manchego cheese, the Gonzalezes use mozzarella. Serve this delicious dish with your favorite Mexican rice.

Tomato-Chile Sauce

3 large beefsteak tomatoes or 2 cups drained canned tomatoes

½ cup chopped white onion

1 chicken bouillon cube

1 garlic clove, peeled

1 tablespoon vegetable oil

Salt and freshly ground black pepper

Chiles Rellenos

6 large poblano (also called ancho) chiles

4 ounces mozzarella cheese, cut into 6 sticks (about ½ inch wide and 3 inches long)

Vegetable oil, for deep-frying

5 large eggs, separated

½ cup all-purpose flour

1 To make the sauce, position a broiler rack about 6 inches from the source of heat and preheat the broiler. Place the tomatoes on a broiler pan and broil, turning occasionally, until the skins are blackened and blistered, about 8 minutes. (This can also be done outside on a grill.) Transfer to a bowl and let cool. Peel and seed the tomatoes, and coarsely chop the flesh.

2 Puree the tomatoes, 1 cup water, the onion, the bouillon cube, and the garlic in a blender. Heat the oil in a medium saucepan over medium-high heat. Carefully pour in the tomato mixture (it will splatter) and bring to a boil. Reduce the heat to medium and simmer briskly, stirring often, until reduced by about one-fourth. Season with salt and pepper. Reduce the heat to very low and cover to keep warm.

3 Meanwhile, place the chiles on a broiler pan. Broil, turning occasionally, until the chile skins are blackened and blistered, about 8 minutes. Transfer to a bowl, cover with plastic wrap, and let stand for 20 minute or until cool enough to handle.

4 If you have sensitive skin, wear protective gloves for this step. Peel off the blackened chile skins. Working with 1 chile at a time, remove the stem and the seeds from inside the chile, trying to keep the chile intact. Slip a piece of cheese inside and close the top of the chile with a wooden toothpick.

5 Pour oil into a large, deep skillet to come halfway up the sides and heat over high heat until it reaches 350°F. Line a baking sheet with a paper bag and place it near the stove.

6 Beat the egg whites in a medium bowl with an electric mixer on high speed until soft peaks form. Beat the yolks in another bowl until pale yellow and thickened, about 1 minute. Using a rubber spatula, fold the yolks into the whites. Spread the flour in a shallow dish. Place the egg batter and flour near the deep-frying skillet.

7 Coat each chile in flour, shaking off the excess. Dip in the egg batter, letting the excess drip back into the bowl. Carefully place in the hot oil. (If the pan is large enough to hold the chiles without crowding, fry them all at once; otherwise, cook in two batches.) Deep-fry until golden brown, about 2 minutes. Using a slotted spoon, remove to the paper to drain briefly.

8 Place each chile on a plate. Spoon the warm sauce over and serve immediately.

> "In baseball, it is really important to live in the moment. There are going to be good moments and bad moments. You learn to turn the page."

ROY HALLADAY

PITCHER PHILADELPHIA PHILLIES

★ Roy Halladay is not only a seven-time All-Star and the 2003 American League and 2010 National League Cy Young winner, but he has also accomplished the rare and virtually impossible feat of pitching a perfect game. He shares this ultimate experience with just nineteen other pitchers in the history of the game.

"It was surprising," says Halladay. "You know, what really struck me afterward is how much I actually enjoyed it during the game. For me, I'll always remember doing it and not so much the celebrations or anything after that. I'll always remember actually being on the field and the first couple of seconds afterward with [catcher Carlos] Ruiz."

Another moment with Ruiz that Halladay is sure to remember occurred on October 6, 2010, when he became only the second pitcher in history to throw a no-hitter in the post-season. By completely blanking the Cincinnati Reds that day, he also joined the ranks of only four other pitchers who have thrown two no-hitters in the same season.

Nearly a decade earlier in his career, Halladay's pitching performances were a long way from perfect and he was sent down to the Minor Leagues. Now one of the greatest pitchers in baseball, Halladay cites his return to the Minor Leagues as a life-changing experience professionally: "For me, it was kind of a learning process when I had to go back to A ball and work my way back. I think that period of a month and a half shaped my career. Had I not gone back, I would not have had the chance to kind of reassess myself, reinvent, and learn new things. That month and a half really changed my career."

The extremely talented and driven Halladay brings experience and the right approach to the mound. "I think, more than anything, your work habits and trying to stay positive are a big part of baseball, especially knowing that at some point you're going to fail," he says. "For me, having the right attitude going into it helps you bounce back from those things and helps you to continue to move forward. If you go in and you get defeated easily, it is tough to make it very far."

Known for his self-imposed, highly disciplined workouts, Halladay breaks a sweat a lot earlier than his teammates and coaches, arriving at the ballpark hours before everyone else. Even during spring training, he gets to the ballpark at 5 a.m. "In the spring we are on the field at 9 a.m., and I like working out before. I feel better if I've got my work done early. Plus I have more energy early on than I do after the workout," he explains. Having a consistent regimen is equally significant for Halladay. He says, "For me, the routine part of it is important; that way I know how I am going to feel every time. It's hard to anticipate how you're going to feel going into each game, and I think the more you have a regular pattern, the more your body gets used to that and you know exactly how you're going to feel going out."

Halladay continues to work hard for the Phillies, but his off-the-field time is devoted to his wife and two sons: "Family time to me is extremely important. I probably enjoy that the most and get the most satisfaction out of that." He adds, "Knowing that I am doing things the right way and that my kids are starting to pick up on that is pretty satisfying to me."

Halladay's own upbringing in Denver, Colorado, included homemade family meals. "Lasagna was one of my favorites growing up," he recalls fondly. "You know, that's what you always asked for on birthdays. My mom would make lasagna and she'd make chocolate cake—with chocolate frosting."

Today, Halladay enjoys some new favorites made by his wife, Brandy. "She makes tacos; I love those," he says. Though Halladay does not cook, he says, "I do Thanksgiving. I'll do the turkey on the rotisserie. That's my specialty." And as for dessert, Halladay's favorite is "lava chocolate cake with vanilla ice cream and hot chocolate syrup."

During the season, Halladay does not have any food rituals, but he knows his body needs fuel before a game: "I can't eat five or six hours before, so I drink a lot of protein shakes within an hour of the game." His protein shakes often include fruit, yogurt, and a spoonful of peanut butter. And he is a green tea convert, even keeping a stock of his favorite tea at the ballpark.

Eating is "not as regimented during the off-season," Halladay says. "During baseball, you're making sure you get breakfast and making sure you're eating something at least five or six times a day, if you can. And during the winter it is a lot more unpredictable." When not pitching, Halladay enjoys more than the occasional frozen indulgence: He reveals that his refrigerator is always thoroughly stocked with ice cream. "People would be surprised to find all the ice cream in my kitchen."

During the winter months, when Halladay has a break from the pitcher's mound, he likes to immerse himself in nonbaseball activities. "I have numerous hobbies," he says. "I'll have five every winter, such as fly-fishing, Ping-Pong, pool, and welding. I built a go-cart dune-buggy thing one winter. For some reason, I get hooked into something for a couple months and that's all I can do for two months until it's almost overkill, and then I find something else and move on."

Luckily for baseball, Halladay has been hooked on pitching for a long, long time.

GRILLED TURKEY WITH SAGE GRAVY

MAKES 8–12 SERVINGS

★ Roy Halladay fires up the backyard grill to cook his family's Thanksgiving bird. Grilling allows the turkey to pick up an incredible smoky flavor. I've also included a method for making pan gravy from the drippings. Make this and it will probably become your family stand-by for holiday turkeys. If you don't have a grill, you can roast the turkey on a rack in a roasting pan, uncovered, in a 325°F oven for the same cooking time.

1 whole turkey, about 12 pounds

3 cups chopped onions

6 tablespoons (¾ stick) unsalted butter, at room temperature, plus melted butter for the gravy

Salt and freshly ground black pepper

1 tablespoon vegetable oil, plus more for the rack

1½ quarts canned reduced-sodium chicken broth

½ cup plus 1 tablespoon all-purpose flour

2 teaspoons chopped fresh sage

1 Remove the giblets, neck, and lumps of fat from the tail area; cover and set aside. Rinse the turkey inside and out and pat dry with paper towels. Fill the neck cavity with some of the chopped onion and pin the neck skin to the back with a wooden or metal skewer. Tuck the turkey wing tips behind the turkey shoulders. Place the ends of the drumsticks in the metal or plastic holder, or tie together with butchers' twine. Rub the turkey with 6 tablespoons butter and season all over with the salt and pepper. Add 1 cup of the chopped onion to the body cavity. Place the turkey on an oiled roasting rack in a disposable aluminum foil roasting pan. (Do not use a high-quality roasting pan, as the smoke may discolor it.) Let the turkey stand at room temperature while preparing the grill, no longer than 1 hour.

2 Prepare a fire in an outdoor grill. If using a charcoal grill, light 5 pounds of briquettes or charcoal and burn until covered with white ash. Spread into 2 mounds on either side of the grill with an empty area in the center. If using a gas grill, preheat the grill on high, then turn one burner off and the other burner(s) to medium. You want to maintain a grill temperature of 325° to 350°F.

3 Place the reserved fat in the pan. Place the turkey in the pan over the empty (or turned-off) area of the grill. (If using a charcoal grill, place an oven thermometer next to the pan.) Cover and grill with the lid closed as much as possible, keeping the grill's temperature around 350°F, until an instant-read thermometer inserted in the thickest part of the thigh, not touching a bone, reaches 170°F, about 2¾ hours. If using a charcoal grill, add 10 unlighted briquettes or charcoal chunks to the pan about every 45 minutes. Occasionally during grilling, tilt the bird so the juices run out of the cavity into the pan. Allow the juices to reduce and turn dark brown, as they will add color to the gravy.

4 While the turkey is grilling, make turkey stock. In a large saucepan, heat the 1 tablespoon oil over medium-high heat. Using a heavy knife or cleaver, chop the neck into 2-inch chunks. Add the neck, gizzard, and heart (discard the liver) to the saucepan and cook, turning occasionally, until browned, about 6 minutes. Add the remaining chopped onion and cook until softened, about 3 minutes. Add the broth and 2 cups water and bring to a simmer. Reduce the heat to low and simmer for 2 hours. Drain, discard the solids, and set the stock aside.

5 When the turkey is done, transfer to a platter and let rest for 20 to 30 minutes. Set the roasting pan aside. Strain the pan juices into a fat separator or glass bowl. Let stand for 3 minutes so the fat rises to the surface. Pour (or skim) the pan juices into a 2-quart measuring cup. Add stock as needed to make 1½ quarts.

6 Measure the fat. You should have 9 tablespoons; add melted butter as needed. In a medium saucepan, heat the fat (and butter, if using) over medium heat. Whisk in the flour and let bubble for 1 minute. Whisk

in the stock mixture and bring to a boil. Reduce the heat to medium-low and simmer the gravy base for 5 minutes.

7 Place the foil pan over low heat. Pour the gravy base mixture into the foil pan and scrape up any browned bits in the pan with a rubber spatula, taking care not to pierce the pan. Return the gravy to the saucepan and add the sage. Simmer, whisking often, for 3 minutes longer, until slightly thickened. If the gravy is too thick, add more stock. Season carefully with salt and pepper.

8 Carve the turkey and serve with the gravy.

PEANUT BUTTER AND CHOCOLATE SHAKE

MAKES 1 SERVING

★ Roy Halladay isn't the only ballplayer who downs a protein-rich shake before a game. This version is particularly lip-smacking, and it's worthy of making any time you crave a smooth and creamy cold beverage. Use a really ripe banana and the shake will be naturally sweetened. And don't skip the step of dissolving the cocoa powder, as the boiling water opens up its flavor.

1 tablespoon boiling water (the easiest way is to heat cold water in the microwave)

2 teaspoons unsweetened cocoa powder

¼ cup skim or whole milk, or more as needed

1 very ripe banana, peeled and thinly sliced

1 large scoop (about ½ cup) frozen vanilla yogurt or ice cream

3 tablespoons crunchy peanut butter

Mix the boiling water and cocoa together in a small custard cup or coffee cup until smooth. Pour into a blender. Add the milk, banana, yogurt, and peanut butter. Blend, stopping the machine to scrape down the sides and adding more milk as needed to reach the desired thickness, until smooth. Pour into a tall glass and serve immediately.

PERFECT GREEN TEA

MAKES 1 SERVING

★ Roy Halladay likes everything about green tea, from its healthful profile to its bracing flavor that revitalizes and soothes at the same time. It is simple to prepare if you follow the tips outlined below. There are many varieties of green tea to choose from, but enjoy it pure without added flavorings. Try Japanese sencha (my personal favorite) or Chinese Dragonwell.

1 cup cold water

1 green tea bag

Heat 1 cup cold water in a saucepan or teakettle over high heat to the point just before the water reaches a boil. (A saucepan allows you to see the water's progress more easily than a kettle.) Drop a green tea bag into a mug and fill the mug with water. Let stand for 3 minutes—no longer, or the tea will become bitter. Remove and discard the tea bag. Let the tea cool for 1 minute. Put your feet up, relax, and enjoy one sip at a time.

MOLTEN CHOCOLATE LAVA CAKES

MAKES 6 SERVINGS

★ Gooey and decadent, these warm individual cakes with their saucy insides are a can't-resist dessert for Roy Halladay. They are great for dinner parties, too, because they can be made a few hours ahead and baked just before serving. Don't worry if they get a little overbaked: You can serve them as warm chocolate brownie cakes, and no one will know the difference.

12 tablespoons (1½ sticks) unsalted butter, plus more for the ramekins

6 ounces semisweet or bittersweet chocolate, finely chopped

3 large eggs plus 3 large yolks

⅓ cup packed light brown sugar

1 teaspoon vanilla extract

1 tablespoon all-purpose flour, plus more for the ramekins

Vanilla ice cream, for serving

1 Position a rack in the center of the oven and preheat the oven to 425°F. Lightly butter the insides of six ½-cup ramekins or custard cups. Dust the insides with flour and tap out the excess flour.

2 Melt the butter in a medium saucepan over medium-low heat. Remove from the heat and add the chocolate. Let stand 2 minutes, then whisk until smooth.

3 Beat the eggs, yolks, and brown sugar with an electric mixer on high speed until light in color and texture, about 3 minutes. Beat in the vanilla. Add the chocolate mixture, sprinkle with the flour, and fold together with a rubber spatula. Divide evenly among the ramekins. (The cakes can be prepared to this point and refrigerated for up to 4 hours. Remove from the refrigerator 1 hour before baking.)

4 Place the ramekins on a baking sheet. Bake until the top of the cake looks set and the center still jiggles a little when the baking sheet is shaken, about 10 minutes.

5 Remove from the oven and let stand for 1 minute. Carefully run a dinner knife around the inside of one of the ramekins. Place a dessert plate on top of the ramekin. Invert the ramekin and plate together, and give the pair a firm shake to dislodge and unmold the cake onto the plate. Remove the ramekin. Repeat with remaining ramekins. Serve the cakes at once, with a small scoop of vanilla ice cream.

> "Since I was twelve years old, I loved baseball more than any other sport and I played everything. I played football, basketball, baseball, soccer, ran track, and did everything I possibly could. I loved baseball the most."

JOSH HAMILTON

OUTFIELDER TEXAS RANGERS

★ Josh Hamilton's amazing athleticism enabled him to master nearly any sport. But baseball was his future, a discovery he made in grade school. Born and raised in Raleigh, North Carolina, Hamilton credits his older brother as his biggest influence in sports, especially baseball. "When I was seven, I played with my brother—who was four years older than me," he recalls. "I played with nine through twelve year olds, and that kind of helped my confidence and helped start things as far as having that feeling I could do anything athletically. I held my own. I hit a home run off a twelve-year-old kid. It was really fun. My brother always included me and always allowed me to play with him and his friends, and he never took it easy on me—which was a good thing."

And Hamilton's knack for the game earned him a lofty reward when he was no more than a teenager. On June 2, 1999, his father's birthday, Hamilton was chosen as Major League Baseball's number-one draft selection. Known for hitting monstrous home runs, Hamilton seemed to be an All-American superstar in the making. But unfortunately, while in the Minor Leagues, his baseball career was alarmingly curtailed by a dark period of substance abuse that nearly cost him his life and kept him out of baseball for a couple years.

Armed with a strong will, a prevailing faith, and unflagging family support, Hamilton has put turbulent days behind him and made his Major League debut in 2007 with the Cincinnati Reds—a remarkable feat in a game that affords very few second chances. He says, "I got a little taste of success being drafted out of high school, but my priorities being out of order prevented me from getting to where I wanted to go, so when I found those priorities and put them in the right spot and where they needed to be—God first, family second, and everything else after that—that's when everything started coming together."

"It's all about a homemade meal. If it is made with love, it's going to taste a little better."

"Coming together" may be an understatement for the Texas Rangers outfielder, who was recently voted the 2010 MVP and has made three All Star appearances and garnered two Silver Slugger awards. His record-breaking slugfest in the 2008 All-Star Home Run Derby was a transforming moment just one year after his comeback and ascent to the Majors. "The Home Run Derby was a memorable experience for me because I had my family there," he recalls. "After everything that had happened and what we had gone through together, that was pretty special, and the way the crowd in New York responded to what was going on, it was just awesome, an awesome time."

Not only has Hamilton survived the repercussions of a four-year battle with drug abuse but, in an ongoing effort to help others, he also chronicled his very personal ordeal in a profound memoir, *Beyond Belief*. Today, he continues to share his life experience with others through speaking engagements and lectures across the country. Ultimately, Hamilton hopes "to be a good ambassador for the game and take time with people and take time with fans." He adds, "A lot of guys lose perspective on why they are really here. The fans are the reason we are able to do what we do." While growing up, Hamilton was a fan of Cal Ripken Jr., Paul O'Neill, and Tony Gwynn. "I like those guys because I liked the way they carried themselves," he says.

During the season, Hamilton and his wife, Katie, live outside of Dallas with their three young daughters. While Hamilton's focus remains on baseball, family time is most important to him when he is not on the field. On a rare day off, he enjoys taking his daughters fishing or having fun on the backyard trampoline. Recently Hamilton developed an interest in photography, and he enjoys photographing nature scenes and animals. "I love being outdoors," says Hamilton. Family time also extends to an evening game followed by dinner together. In addition to going to the ballpark to watch her husband's games, Katie prepares a homemade dinner for her family beforehand. "When I am playing, Katie fixes dinner for me every night after the game," he says proudly. "Everybody else eats in the clubhouse and they go home, but Katie has a meal for me when I go home. She also goes to my games, so she lays out what she has to do to get it ready before the game. Any time we can get the kids together, say our prayers, and have a meal together, it is pretty special. It doesn't happen nowadays with people."

Hamilton's notion of delicious food consists of Southern meals from his childhood. "Good old country dishes," he says. "And things that came right out of the garden. There is something about it that makes it better." Some of his favorites among the dishes Katie makes are pork loin and sweet potato casserole. His grandmother, whose memorable meals also top his list, taught him a thing or two in the kitchen. "My grandmother taught me how to cook eggs, scrambled eggs, over easy, or whatever, and she taught me how to make

mashed potatoes and gravy," he says. But most of all for Hamilton, "It's all about a homemade meal. If it is made with love, it's going to taste a little better. And if my wife makes it or my grandmother makes it, there is something different about it. It is so much better."

For sweets, his two favorites are "the fudge my aunt fixes for me and homemade chocolate chip cookies—can't be soft, can't be too firm, have to be just right." And he cites homemade sweet tea as his special treat on a hot Texas afternoon.

Texas weather can be unpredictable, including bursts of heavy rain, but Hamilton is usually prepared. He notes, "I like watching the Weather Channel. They play music and if there is a storm in the area, the alerts come on. We live in an area where there are lots of storms." Katie adds, "He goes to sleep with it on every single night." Thankfully, Hamilton has weathered storms both on and off the field, earning the admiration and respect of baseball fans everywhere.

SWEET TEA

MAKES 4–6 SERVINGS

★ Southern-style iced tea is always sweetened and always made with orange pekoe black tea. Josh Hamilton's wife, Katie, likes to make a refreshing pitcher of sweet tea on extra-warm days in Texas. She prefers to use decaffeinated tea, which is equally good. Either way, the tea must be brewed strong to keep its flavor when it is later diluted with ice. Add more or less sugar to suit your taste, and serve with lemon slices.

6 orange pekoe tea bags
¾ cup sugar

1   Bring 2½ cups water to a boil in a saucepan over high heat. Remove saucepan from the heat and add the tea bags. Let steep for 10 minutes.

2   Remove and discard the tea bags. Add the sugar and stir to dissolve. Add 2½ cups ice water to the saucepan and stir well. Pour into a pitcher. Serve in tall glasses over ice.

HOMEMADE WHITE BREAD

MAKES 2 LOAVES OR 16 ROLLS

★ Josh Hamilton's wife, Katie, sent me this recipe with the following note: "This is the bread recipe that I make and LOVE!" That's quite an endorsement. She's right, too. What can beat a loaf of warm, just-baked bread? Katie uses a heavy-duty stand mixer to make her bread, but it can also be kneaded by hand.

2 cups warm (105°–115°F) water

2 tablespoons sugar or honey

2¾ teaspoons active dry yeast

6 cups bread flour, or as needed

2 teaspoons salt

2 tablespoons unsalted butter, at room temperature, plus more for the bowl and pans

1 To make the dough with a mixer, combine the warm water, sugar, and yeast in the bowl of a heavy-duty stand mixer. Let stand until the mixture shows signs of life (it will be foamy or slightly bubbling), about 10 minutes. Stir to dissolve the yeast. Add 2½ cups of flour and the salt. Attach the bowl to the mixer and fit with the paddle attachment. With the mixer on low speed, gradually add enough of the flour to make a soft dough that comes away from the bowl. Replace the paddle attachment with the dough hook. Mix on medium speed, adding more flour as needed, until the dough is smooth and supple, about 8 minutes. The dough will be slightly tacky—do not add too much flour.

To make the dough by hand, combine the warm water, sugar, and yeast in a large bowl. Let stand until the mixture shows signs of life (it will be foamy or slightly bubbling), about 10 minutes. Stir to dissolve the yeast. Stir in 1 cup flour and the salt. Gradually stir in enough of the flour to make a dough that cannot be stirred. Turn out onto a well-floured work surface. Knead, adding more flour as necessary, until the dough is smooth and supple, about 10 minutes. Do

not add too much flour—if the dough is slightly tacky but doesn't stick to the work surface, the flour amount is correct.

2 Lightly butter a large bowl. Shape the dough into a ball. Place in the bowl and turn to coat with the butter, leaving the ball smooth side up. Cover the bowl with plastic wrap. Let stand in a warm, draft-free place until doubled in volume, about 1 hour.

3 Lightly butter two 8½ x 4½-inch loaf pans. Cut the dough in half. Shape each half into a loaf to fit the pan. Place each, seam side down, in a pan, patting the dough to fill the corners. Cover with plastic wrap and let stand in a warm, draft-free place until the dough begins to dome over the top of the pans, about 40 minutes.

4 Position a rack in the center of the oven and preheat to 350°F. Uncover the pans and bake until the loaves are golden brown and the bottoms sound hollow when tapped (remove a loaf to check), about 35 minutes. Let cool in the pans on a wire cake rack for 5 minutes. Turn loaves out onto the rack, turn right side up, and let cool for at least 15 minutes before slicing.

DINNER ROLLS: Cut the dough into 16 equal pieces. Shape each into a ball. Lightly butter two 8-inch round cake pans. Arrange 8 balls in each pan, smooth sides up. Cover with plastic wrap and let stand until balls are doubled in size, about 40 minutes. Uncover pans and bake rolls at 350°F until golden brown, 20 to 25 minutes. Remove from the pans and serve warm.

SLOW-COOKED PULLED PORK SANDWICHES

MAKES 8 SERVINGS

★ This is Josh Hamilton's favorite sandwich to eat with his family, especially when he comes home after a game. Katie must like making it, too, because it is a classic slow-cooker recipe that needs very little attention. The payoff is meltingly tender pork in a sweet sauce. To round out the meal Southern-style, serve the sandwiches with coleslaw, baked beans, or fries.

1 3½-pound boneless pork shoulder or butt roast, rind and excess fat trimmed

Salt and freshly ground black pepper

2 18–22-ounce bottles of your favorite barbecue sauce

8 sesame seed buns, toasted

1 Lightly season the pork with salt and pepper. Place in a slow cooker insert, add the barbecue sauce, and cover. Cook on low until the pork is fork-tender, 8–9 hours.

2 Skim off any fat from the sauce surface. Transfer the pork to a carving board. Let stand for 5 minutes. Using two forks, shred the pork, discarding any excess fat. Return to the slow cooker.

3 Heap the meat and sauce onto the buns and serve hot.

SWEET POTATO CASSEROLE

MAKES 8–10 SERVINGS

★ There are few dishes that say American cooking more than sweet potato casserole. Katie Hamilton makes this special dish for husband Josh and their daughters. Her casserole is full of irresistible flavors and is topped with an out-of-this-world layer of pecan streusel. Serve this alongside your holiday turkey or ham for a meal you won't forget.

Casserole

2 pounds medium orange-fleshed sweet potatoes

½ cup sugar

½ cup whole milk

4 tablespoons (½ stick) unsalted butter, melted, plus more for the dish

2 large eggs, beaten

1 teaspoon vanilla extract

½ teaspoon salt

Topping

1 cup packed light brown sugar

1 cup (4 ounces) coarsely chopped pecans

⅓ cup all-purpose flour

5 tablespoons unsalted butter, melted

1 Pierce each sweet potato a few times with a fork. Microwave on high, turning halfway through cooking, until tender, about 15 minutes. (Or roast the sweet potatoes in a roasting pan in a preheated 400°F oven until tender, about 1 hour.) Let cool until easy to handle.

2 Position a rack in the center of the oven and preheat the oven to 350°F. Lightly butter an 11½ x 8-inch baking dish.

3 Peel the sweet potatoes. Transfer the flesh to a large bowl. Add the sugar, milk, melted butter, eggs, vanilla, and salt. Mash with an electric mixer set on low speed until smooth. Spread in the dish.

4 To make the topping, using your fingertips, work the brown sugar, pecans, flour, and melted butter together in a medium bowl until combined. Sprinkle evenly over the sweet potato mixture.

5 Bake until the casserole is bubbling around the edges, about 30 minutes. Let cool for 5 minutes. Serve warm.

> "Discipline, confidence, and respect. This was my motto back when I was in college."

ON THE MENU

LEMON AND HERB CHICKEN BREASTS

COBB SALAD WITH BALSAMIC SHALLOT VINAIGRETTE

MACARONI AND CHEESE WITH BROCCOLI

RYAN HOWARD

FIRST BASEMAN PHILADELPHIA PHILLIES

★ A credible yet simple mantra—"discipline, confidence, and respect"—is a constant inspiration for All-Star first baseman Ryan Howard. A big believer in these three powerful words, Howard had them tattooed along the massive biceps of his right arm, a compelling reminder.

Howard made his start in 2001 as the Philadelphia Phillies' first-round draft selection. Four years later, he won the National League Rookie of the Year Award, and his outstanding performance didn't stop there. With his notable power hitting, Howard was a major contributor to the Phillies' 2008 World Series championship campaign. His numerous individual achievements include being a three-time All-Star and the recipient of the Silver Slugger and National League MVP awards. And as another recent accolade, Howard has entered the Philadelphia Phillies record books for power and consistency, with a fifth consecutive season of more than thirty home runs and one hundred RBIs.

"Laid back" isn't the first term that comes to mind when describing one of the fiercest sluggers in the game, but "that's just kind of how I've always been—just very laid back," says Howard. A two-time National League home run leader, Howard was the fastest hitter in Major League history to reach one hundred home runs. His killer hitting can be traced back to his childhood. He recalls, "I guess there was this home run everyone was talking about, me hitting this Red Lobster building when I was twelve. They said it was a 430-foot straight shot or something like that."

"I eat a lot of organic food mixed in with my workout. You know, just eating more healthily."

What continues to get his mind and body in sync with hitting monstrous homers? Howard has a distinct routine when he is at the plate. He says, "I kind of do my little bat routine when I get up to the plate and do a little stretch, take two swings, create a line, tap the place twice, once on each side of the plate, and go into my crouch." And his stance at the plate before taking a pitch is unmistakably Howard—deliberate and unique, with his bat firmly grasped in his right hand while momentarily pointing towards the outfield.

Howard, who is in his early thirties, grew up in St. Louis, Missouri, and is one of four children. He recalls attending his first Major League game at age seven. "It was definitely a Cardinals game," he recalls. Though he now calls Philadelphia home, he remains close to family and friends back in St. Louis: "I would definitely say my family and friends keep me grounded. I'll see a few friends when I go back to St. Louis. I see high school friends and old college coaches." But Howard is closest to his fraternal twin brother, Corey, who lives with him in Philadelphia. Before Major League Baseball came calling, Howard and his brother shared many school activities, including playing the trombone together in the school marching band. "My brother was a little bit better," Howard says. "I actually wanted to play the sax, but my band teacher told me I had long arms so I should play the trombone. Plus, I think she wanted to even out the band and already had sax players, so I said all right." The twins also have an older brother, and Howard, who is 6-foot-4, is quick to state, "I'm the smallest of the three."

Away from the baseball diamond, Howard enjoys spending time with his son, traveling, reading books, and spending time with a few teammates. He says, "The off-season is usually spent doing stuff with the guys." One of his favorite places to travel to is Hawaii. "I play in [teammate] Shane Victorino's charity golf tournament every year in Hawaii, and I spend a lot of time with my son. We go to Disney World. I'm pretty simple. Just try to live life and be happy."

Back in the 2009 off-season, Howard revamped his eating habits to include healthier foods. "I eat a lot of organic food mixed in with my workout. You know, just eating more healthily," he says. "I just needed to change it up, change up my diet because while playing baseball and traveling it is hard to eat healthily." Since changing his diet, Howard has lost nearly thirty pounds. His secret to maintaining his new physique is "being consistent and going on a run with it," he says.

Before heading to the ballpark, Howard starts his day with a full breakfast: "I eat oatmeal and an egg-white omelet. I put everything in my omelet—mushrooms, peppers, onions, sausage, and bacon." Though Howard is not a natural in the kitchen, he admits to a few culinary skills. "Every once in a while, not a lot, I grill up some chicken," he says. He

does enjoy eating a traditional cobb salad and declares broccoli his favorite vegetable. But mac 'n' cheese will always remain number-one for Howard. While growing up, he and his siblings frequently indulged in Mom's specialty and, as a result, he says, "I am always a big fan of macaroni and cheese." And Philadelphia baseball followers will always be big fans of first baseman Ryan Howard.

COBB SALAD WITH BALSAMIC SHALLOT VINAIGRETTE

MAKES 4 SERVINGS

★ It is a salad, but cobb salad was never meant to be a healthful or low-fat dish. Because Ryan Howard is a conscientious eater, however, this version is a lighter version that still packs some punch from the familiar flavors of the original. Use reduced-fat blue cheese and turkey bacon, serve the dressing on the side, and dig into this classic mega-salad.

Balsamic Shallot Vinaigrette

¼ cup balsamic vinegar

½ teaspoon salt

¼ teaspoon freshly ground black pepper

¾ cup extra-virgin olive oil

2 tablespoons minced shallots

Salad

2 8-ounce skinless, boneless chicken breast halves

½ teaspoon salt

¼ teaspoon freshly ground black pepper

2 teaspoons extra-virgin olive oil

2 8-ounce romaine hearts, washed, dried, and torn into bite-sized pieces

2 large ripe tomatoes, seeded and diced

2 ripe avocados, pitted, peeled, and diced

8 strips turkey bacon, cooked and coarsely chopped

2 hard-boiled eggs, coarsely chopped

1 cup (4 ounces) crumbled reduced-fat blue cheese

1 To make the vinaigrette, combine the vinegar, salt, and pepper in a blender. With the machine running, gradually add the oil. Add the shallots and pulse briefly to combine. Pour into a serving bowl and set aside.

2 Pound each chicken breast half between 2 heavy-duty plastic bags with a flat meat pounder to an even ½-inch thickness. Season with the salt and pepper. Heat the oil in a large nonstick skillet over medium-high heat. Add the chicken and cook, turning halfway through cooking, until golden brown on both sides, about 6 minutes. Add ¼ cup water, reduce the heat to medium-low, and cover. Simmer until the chicken feels firm when pressed in the center, about 8 minutes. Uncover, increase the heat to high, and cook until the liquid is evaporated and the chicken is sizzling, about 1 minute. Transfer chicken to a carving board and let cool. Cut the chicken into bite-sized pieces.

3 Spread the lettuce on a large platter. Top with the chicken, tomatoes, avocados, bacon, hard-boiled eggs, and blue cheese arranged in rows. Serve immediately, with the vinaigrette passed on the side.

LEMON AND HERB CHICKEN BREASTS

MAKES 4 SERVINGS

★ Howard is a self-proclaimed noncook, but he does occasionally prepare some chicken on his backyard grill. There is only one secret to this citrus-and-herb-scented marinade: Do not marinate the chicken for longer than six hours, or the acids in the lemon juice will toughen the chicken flesh.

¼ cup freshly squeezed lemon juice

2 garlic cloves, minced

1 teaspoon dried thyme

1 teaspoon dried sage

1 teaspoon sweet or smoked paprika

1 teaspoon salt

½ teaspoon freshly ground black pepper

2 bay leaves

½ cup extra-virgin olive oil

4 8-ounce skinless, boneless chicken breast halves

1 Whisk the lemon juice, garlic, thyme, sage, paprika, salt, pepper, and bay leaves together in a medium bowl. Gradually whisk in the oil. Pour into a large zip-top plastic bag.

2 Pound each chicken breast half between 2 heavy-duty plastic bags with a flat meat pounder to an even ½-inch thickness. Add the chicken to the marinade and close the bag. Refrigerate, turning occasionally, for at least 2 hours and up to 6 hours.

3 Prepare a medium fire in an outdoor grill. If using a charcoal grill, let the coals burn until you can hold your hand just above the cooking grate for about 3 seconds. If using a gas grill, preheat on high, then adjust to medium. Place the chicken on the grill and cover. Grill the chicken, flipping it over halfway through cooking, until it feels firm when pressed in the center, about 12 minutes. If the chicken drips and causes flare-ups, move it to a cooler part of the grill, not directly over a source of heat. Serve hot.

MACARONI AND CHEESE WITH BROCCOLI

MAKES 4–6 SERVINGS

★ One of the most delicious dishes on the planet is macaroni and cheese. For Ryan Howard, as for many people, it evokes memories of home. It is a tasty coincidence that Ryan Howard's favorite dish and number-one vegetable go so well together.

6 tablespoons (¾ stick) unsalted butter, plus more for the dish

¼ cup all-purpose flour

3 cups whole milk, heated

4 cups (1 pound) sharp or mild cheddar, shredded

½ teaspoon dry mustard

3 cups bite-size broccoli florets

1 pound elbow macaroni

Salt and freshly ground black pepper

2 cups cornflakes

1 Position a rack in the center of the oven and preheat the oven to 350ºF. Lightly butter a 13 x 9-inch baking dish.

2 Bring a large pot of lightly salted water to a boil over high heat.

3 Meanwhile, melt 4 tablespoons butter in a large saucepan over low heat. Whisk in the flour and let bubble without browning for 1 minute. Whisk in the milk and increase the heat to medium. Bring to a boil, whisking often. Remove from the heat, add the cheddar and mustard, and whisk until the cheese melts. Set aside.

4 Add the broccoli to the boiling water and cook just until bright green but still crisp, about 2 minutes. Using a wire spider or a sieve, lift the broccoli out of the water and transfer to a bowl of cold water. Add the macaroni to the boiling water and cook according to the package directions until al dente. Do not overcook. Drain well in a colander. Pour the broccoli over the macaroni to drain. Return the macaroni and broccoli to the pot. Add the sauce and stir to combine. Season with salt and pepper.

5 Spread the macaroni mixture in the baking dish. Toss the corn flakes and remaining 2 tablespoons butter in a small bowl. Sprinkle over the macaroni mixture. Bake until bubbling, about 20 minutes. Serve hot.

DEREK JETER

SHORTSTOP NEW YORK YANKEES

★ As the captain of the New York Yankees, Derek Jeter has an unrivaled reputation that resonates through baseball. With a Major League career that has been nothing short of historic, he has spent his entire professional baseball career with the Bronx Bombers. Yet, Jeter has the respect of a fan base beyond his pinstripes. Throughout his fifteen-year career, his performance on the diamond has earned him numerous awards and well-deserved recognition, including eleven All-Star appearances and multiple Gold Glove and Silver Slugger awards. Today, Jeter stands alone as the Yankees' all-time hit leader, having surpassed Lou Gehrig's record in September 2009. After years of on-field individual achievements, however, Jeter's most unforgettable moments are the team's five World Series wins during his tenure. And like a true professional, the perennial All-Star is set on bringing home another championship.

Jeter spent his childhood surrounded by a large group of aunts and uncles. His mother is one of fourteen children, including four adopted siblings. "My grandparents used to live in New Jersey, and my grandmother still lives there. I grew up in Michigan, but my summers were spent in New Jersey," he says. During one of his East Coast summers, he attended his first Major League game at Yankee Stadium. Today, Jeter's parents are steadfast fans at Yankee Stadium.

Jeter's love of baseball was stirred early in his life by his father. "My dad played baseball in college, so I always looked up to him. I wanted to be like him," he says. Jeter's Little League days were his most memorable. "I used to love Opening Day. We used to have a little parade and I would dress up in my uniform the night before. I loved the whole parade

"I love buttermilk biscuits."

thing," he reminisces. Many years later, Jeter finds himself enjoying parades once again: He's participated in all five of his team's World Series victory parades held in New York City's Canyon of Heroes.

During his off-hours, Jeter is equally driven and passionate about giving back to his community. In 1996, he established the Turn 2 Foundation, whose mission is to prevent alcohol and drug abuse among kids by helping them "turn to" a healthier way of living. "I was a big Dave Winfield fan, and he was one of the first to have a foundation while he was still playing, and I always thought that was cool when I was younger. I think we should try to help out," says Jeter.

When Jeter is not hard at work, his favorite pastime is watching movies. "I am a big movie person," he says. "All kinds of movies. You know how women buy shoes? Well, I buy movies. I go to the movie theater all the time, too," he says. And when it comes to a movie snack, Jeter is a big fan of chocolate-covered peanuts, gummy bears, and popcorn.

For the most part, Jeter's meals are a balance of healthy eating and his favorite foods. When it comes to cooking, Jeter leaves that particular skill to others. He gives his mother a nod for teaching him how to grill a good steak, but he readily admits that cooking is not his thing: "I don't have the patience for cooking. I prefer eating." His favorite snack to make for himself at home is a bowl of cereal.

Jeter, like many players, eats the same kind of breakfast every game day. And like many professional athletes, he assuredly claims that this is just a preferred routine, not a superstition. "Every morning before a game I eat pancakes and an omelet," says Jeter. Specifically, his pancakes are always plain with syrup and no butter. As for his choice of omelet fixings, Jeter was previously a devotee of the egg-white omelet with ham and cheese but admits that lately he "switches it up" with new ingredients such as broccoli or red and green peppers for a healthier approach to breakfast. And he is very much a coffee lover, but it has to be cappuccino for the All-Star shortstop. After a long day of working out, Jeter enjoys his favorite dinner of chicken Parmesan and biscuits. "I love buttermilk biscuits," he says. And he admits to having a certain weakness for ice cream, especially a combination of vanilla, chocolate, and caramel. Says the Yankee captain, "I could eat chicken Parmesan and ice cream every day."

Jeter's future goals for off the field include learning a foreign language. "There are so many things I'd like to learn. I'd like to be fluent in Spanish. You learn a little bit throughout the years because you play with Latino players, but I'd like to be fluent," says Jeter. And owning a professional baseball team is high on Jeter's list of goals.

Whether he is facing a slider at the plate or a scrum of reporters in the clubhouse, Jeter is accustomed to adeptly handling the spotlight as today's player . . . and perhaps tomorrow's owner.

BUTTERMILK PANCAKES

MAKES ABOUT 15 PANCAKES

★ Derek Jeter has pancakes every day for breakfast, alongside an egg-white omelet. Together they are a sure-fire energy source all morning long. Buttermilk and whipped egg whites combine to make these flapjacks light and fluffy. This recipe makes a good number of pancakes, which will disappear if you have company over. If you're like Derek Jeter and want to eat pancakes again the next day, just save and refrigerate the extra batter in a covered container. If you do this, thin the batter with milk to a pourable consistency before using it.

2 cups all-purpose flour

3 tablespoons sugar

2 teaspoons baking powder

1 teaspoon baking soda

½ teaspoon salt

2½ cups buttermilk

3 large eggs, separated, at room temperature

3 tablespoons unsalted butter, melted

Vegetable oil, for the griddle

Pure maple syrup and unsalted butter, for serving

1 Heat a griddle or large nonstick skillet over medium-high heat. Position a rack in the center of the oven and preheat to 200°F.

2 Sift the flour, sugar, baking powder, baking soda, and salt together into a large bowl. Add the buttermilk, egg yolks, and melted butter and stir just until the dry ingredients are moistened—the batter should be very lumpy.

3 Beat the egg whites in a medium bowl with an electric mixer on high speed until they form soft peaks. Using a rubber spatula, fold the whites into the batter just until combined—the batter should not be completely smooth.

4 Check the griddle's heat: Flick cold water from your fingers onto the griddle. The drops should form tiny, skittering balls. If not, increase the heat and heat the griddle for a minute or so longer. Lightly oil the griddle. Using about ⅓ cup batter for each pancake, pour the batter onto the griddle. Cook until the pancakes' undersides are golden brown, about 1½ minutes. Turn the pancakes and cook until the other sides are browned, about 1 minute more. Adjust the heat as needed, so the pancakes don't brown too quickly. Transfer cooked pancakes to a baking sheet and keep warm in the oven while making the remaining pancakes.

5 Serve pancakes hot, with the maple syrup and butter.

FLAKY SOUTHERN BISCUITS

MAKES 12 BISCUITS

★ Derek Jeter likes freshly baked biscuits whenever he can get them, but they have to be really good. Southern cooks are famous for their light biscuits, and there is a reason. White Lily flour, a brand that is hard to find north of the Mason-Dixon line, has a very low gluten content that translates to tender biscuits. If you can't get it (but before you say you can't, look online), use regular self-rising flour. Throughout the entire biscuit-making procedure, use a light touch, as overhandling is often the downfall of good biscuits.

8 tablespoons (1 stick) chilled unsalted butter, plus more for the baking sheet

3 cups self-rising flour, preferably White Lily

1 tablespoon sugar

1¼ cups buttermilk

1 large egg

1 Position a rack in the center of the oven and pre-heat the oven to 400ºF. Lightly butter a rimmed baking sheet.

2 Melt 1 tablespoon of the butter; set aside. Cut the remaining 7 tablespoons butter into ½-inch cubes.

3 Whisk the flour and sugar together in a medium bowl. Add the cubed butter. Using a pastry cutter or two knives, cut in the butter until the mixture resembles coarse crumbs. Whisk the buttermilk and egg together. Pour into the flour mixture and stir just until combined. Do not overmix. The dough will be moist. Let stand for 10 minutes so the flour can absorb some of the moisture.

4 Turn the dough out onto a well-floured work surface. Using floured hands, pat the dough into a ½-inch-thick round. Using a 3-inch-diameter cookie cutter or an inverted glass, cut out as many biscuits as you can. Gather up the scraps, knead gently to combine, and pat and cut out biscuits to use up all of the dough. Transfer to the baking sheet. Brush the tops lightly with the reserved melted butter.

5 Bake until the biscuits have risen and are golden brown, about 20 minutes. Let cool slightly, then serve warm.

EGG-WHITE OMELET WITH HAM AND CHEESE

MAKES 1 SERVING

★ Derek Jeter tries to incorporate well-balanced meals into his daily routine. For breakfast, he eats an egg-white (rather than whole egg) omelet. He has long enjoyed an omelet with a bit of ham and just a hint of cheese, but lately he has been changing it up with an all-vegetable version that includes broccoli or red and green peppers. Omelets are a great way to start your day and are super-simple to make, whatever ingredients you choose.

1 teaspoon olive oil
4 large egg whites
Pinch of salt
A few grinds black pepper
¼ cup chopped lean ham
¼ cup (1 ounce) shredded cheddar

1 Heat the oil in a nonstick medium skillet over medium-high heat until the skillet is hot. Whisk the egg whites, salt, and pepper together in a bowl until foamy. Pour into the skillet and cook until the mixture has barely begun to set around the edges, about 30 seconds. Using a heatproof spatula, lift the cooked edges and gently push them towards the center, tilting the skillet slightly to allow the liquid egg whites on top to flow underneath, then cook for 30 seconds. Repeat and cook until the eggs are almost completely set but still slightly moist.

2 Sprinkle the ham and cheese over the top of the omelet. Reduce the heat to low and cover. Cook until the cheese is melted and the top of the omelet is set, about 30 seconds.

3 Uncover the skillet. Slide the omelet out of the pan, using the spatula to fold it in half. Serve hot.

JOSH JOHNSON

PITCHER FLORIDA MARLINS

★ Josh Johnson caught the baseball bug at a young age. As a kid watching the Minnesota Twins win the World Series in 1987, he had his baseball epiphany. "I was three years old when they won the World Series and I got to go to the World Series parade," remembers Johnson.

Now, many years later, the Florida Marlins ace still remains a parade enthusiast. When selected for his first All-Star game, he witnessed another memorable baseball procession spilling over with Major League All-Stars. But for this parade, Johnson was a participant and not an observer. "The parade was awesome. People are just lined up along the streets all the way until you got to the stadium. Going to the All-Star Game for the first time and just being a part of it was a career highlight," says Johnson.

Born in Minneapolis, Johnson grew up in Tulsa, Oklahoma. His father is Canadian and his mother is part Chippewa. As the youngest of five boys, each separated in age by just two years, he was influenced by his four siblings early on: "I followed my brothers from day one as far as I can remember. I was with them all the time. I would go to the field with them when they had practices and just followed them around and learned from them." Today the Johnson brothers remain very close.

In 2002, Johnson was a top draft pick, but it wasn't until he was partway through the Minors that he felt he had a chance to get to the Big Leagues. "At first, going through the Minor Leagues was tough because I had a pretty good ERA and pretty good stats, but I couldn't win. I wasn't winning games—then all of a sudden things starting clicking. Ever since then, things just sort of came to me and I've been able to put together winning

"I don't really like ice cream, but I love ice pops. I could eat ice pops all day and eat anything with strawberries."

streaks," he explains. With a turbo-charged 97 mph fastball, a solid work ethic, and a self-assured presence on the mound, Johnson is one of the top hurlers in the game. And at a physically strong six-foot-seven, he has no problem filling the number-one spot in the Marlins' rotation.

While Johnson was growing up, normal dinner hours were nonexistent in the Johnson household. With five boys, there was always a revolving door of activities. "It was constant commotion going on, people in and out with sports and school. My mom would make a big pot of food, set it on the table and say 'it's ready.' Whoever was there to eat would eat, and if there wasn't any left, then you had to make something for yourself. So I learned early that I had to get in there and get it fast," recalls Johnson. As a child, one of Johnson's favorite meals was Navajo tacos. The family fry bread recipe came from his Native American grand-mother, who passed it along to Johnson's mother. Today, when it comes to comfort food, Johnson does not stray far from his Midwestern roots.

Like most professional baseball players, Johnson often eats dinner late at night after a nine-inning game. These days, he and his wife, Heidi, and their two sons enjoy a home-cooked meal together. Johnson freely admits that he prefers simple food. "I don't venture out too much, and for example, I don't eat sushi," he says. "I don't really like ice cream, but I love ice pops. I could eat ice pops all day and eat anything with strawberries," he declares. And he recently discovered a strong liking for artichokes, stuffed or steamed. And as a pre-ferred snack, Johnson admits to eating kosher dill pickles—five or six of them—every day.

On game days when it's his turn in the pitching rotation, Johnson has a definite food routine: "I wake up and pretty much have the same food, and as long as it is working, I stick with it. I eat pancakes and sausages before every game I pitch. I like to eat something nice and heavy. Regular pancakes with butter and syrup. I drink water—no milk, coffee, or juice. Then I usually just hang out and relax."

Even the night before a game follows a food routine. "Spaghetti is always my go-to the night before a game," says Johnson. He is dead serious about eating spaghetti and has been known to consume an entire box on the eve of a pitching appearance.

Johnson is a die-hard golfer in the off-season. "I like to play a lot of golf," he says. "I play around two times a week and go to the driving range four or five times a week. I played Pine Valley, which is ranked the number-one golf course in the world, and my goal, one day, is to play the top one hundred golf courses." But for the All-Star pitcher, golf will always be a distant second in his world of sports. Always, first and foremost, it's baseball, baseball, baseball.

NAVAJO TACOS WITH CHILI-BEEF TOPPING

MAKES 8 SERVINGS

★ This family recipe is from Josh Johnson's mother, Bonnie, who often made this hearty dish for her sons. Instead of a regular tortilla shell, Navajo tacos use fry bread, a common staple in Native American homes. As a busy mom with five sons on the go, Mrs. Johnson used frozen bread dough, and you can, too. Serve with a plentiful selection of toppings—that's what tacos are all about!

Beef and Corn Topping

2 tablespoons olive oil

1 large yellow onion, chopped

2 medium green bell peppers, seeded and chopped

2 garlic cloves, minced

2 pounds ground round (85% lean)

2 tablespoons chili powder

1 16-ounce can tomato sauce

3 cups fresh or thawed frozen corn kernels

Salt and freshly ground black pepper

Tacos

2 pounds thawed frozen bread dough

All-purpose flour, for rolling and stacking the dough rounds

Vegetable oil, for deep-frying

Shredded iceberg lettuce, diced tomatoes, shredded cheddar, sour cream, thick salsa, chopped canned green chiles, and sliced black olives, for serving

1 To make the topping, heat the oil in a large saucepan over medium heat. Add the onion and green peppers and cook, stirring occasionally, until softened, about 5 minutes. Add the garlic and cook until fragrant, about 1 minute. Add the ground round and increase the heat to medium-high. Cook, breaking up the meat with the side of a spoon, until it looses its raw look, about 8 minutes. Drain off the excess fat.

2 Stir in the chili powder. Add the tomato sauce and 1 cup water and bring to a simmer. Reduce the heat to medium-low and cook, stirring occasionally, until the sauce has thickened, about 15 minutes. Stir in the corn and cook until heated through, about 5 minutes. Season with salt and pepper. Reduce the heat to very low, and cover to keep warm.

3 Cut the bread dough into 8 equal pieces. On a lightly floured work surface, roll out each piece into a 7- to 8-inch round. Cut a 2-inch-wide X into the center of each round. Dust each round lightly on both sides with flour. Stack the rounds, slightly overlapping and separated by sheets of wax paper, on a baking sheet.

4 Pour enough oil to come halfway up the sides of a large, heavy skillet and heat over high heat to 350ºF. Line a baking sheet with a paper bag and place near the stove.

5 One at a time, add a bread round to the skillet and deep-fry, turning once, until golden brown, about 1 minute. Using a slotted spoon, transfer to the paper to drain. Cover the bread with a clean kitchen towel to keep the fry bread warm and soft.

6 Spoon the beef topping into a serving bowl. Place the fry bread in a napkin-lined basket. Serve with the lettuce, tomatoes, cheddar, sour cream, salsa, chiles, and olives, letting each person build his or her own taco.

STUFFED ARTICHOKES

MAKES 4 SERVINGS

★ Stuffed artichokes are a newfound favorite dish for Josh Johnson. During spring training in Jupiter, Florida, many MLB players frequent the ever-popular Giuseppe's Italian Restaurant for memorable meals, including scrumptious stuffed artichokes. This great recipe is courtesy of Giuseppe's owner and chef Constantine DeRosa.

Artichokes

⅓ cup all-purpose flour

4 large artichokes, stems cut off

Bread Stuffing

1 15-ounce package (3¼ cups) dried Italian-seasoned bread crumbs

1 cup (4 ounces) shredded mozzarella cheese

1 cup (4 ounces) freshly grated Pecorino Romano, plus more for serving

2 tablespoons finely chopped fresh parsley

12 garlic cloves, 10 whole and 2 minced

¾ cup extra-virgin olive oil, or as needed, plus more for the pan

Salt and freshly ground black pepper

1 quart canned reduced-sodium chicken broth

1 Whisk the flour into 1 gallon water in a large bowl. Working with one artichoke at a time, cut off 1 inch from the top of the leaves. Using scissors, snip off the sharp tip from each leaf. Pull back the leaves to reveal the pale green cone of leaves at the center. Pull out this pale cone of leaves, using a small knife to cut it free at the base, revealing the hairy choke. Using a spoon, scoop out the choke, creating a hollow in the center of the artichoke. Immerse the artichoke in the floury water. Let soak for 1 hour.

2 Position a rack in the center of the oven and preheat the oven to 350°F. Lightly oil a metal roasting pan.

3 Drain and rinse the artichokes from the water. Mix the bread crumbs, mozzarella, Romano, parsley, and minced garlic. Stir in enough of the oil to moisten the stuffing—it should have the texture of wet sand. Season with salt and pepper.

4 Force as much stuffing as possible underneath the artichoke leaves with your fingertip. Use any remaining stuffing to fill the center hollow of each artichoke. Place the artichokes in the roasting pan. Add the whole garlic cloves and the broth. Bring to a simmer over medium heat. Cover the pan tightly with aluminum foil.

5 Bake until a leaf can be easily pulled from an artichoke, about 1½ hours. Uncover the pan and let the artichokes cool slightly. Transfer each artichoke to a deep soup bowl. Spoon about ⅓ cup of the cooking liquid over each, sprinkle with grated Romano, and serve.

TENDER STRAWBERRY SHORTCAKE

MAKES 6–8 SERVINGS

★ There's more than one way to make shortcake. Although the biscuit version has its fans, you can also make a moist and tender sponge cake similar to the individual "Mary Ann"–style shortcakes you find at some bakeries and local grocers. While a true Mary Ann cake has a rim to hold a topping, there's no need to get a special pan; the shortcake will taste just as luscious without it. For Josh Johnson, it all comes down to the strawberries and the strawberry sauce. Hold out until your local berries are in season, and you'll have a winner.

Berries and Sauce

2 pounds fresh strawberries, hulled and sliced

¼ cup sugar, plus more as needed

1 teaspoon freshly squeezed lemon juice

Sponge Cake

1 cup all-purpose flour, plus more for the pan

1 teaspoon baking powder

½ teaspoon salt

8 tablespoons (1 stick) unsalted butter, at room temperature, plus more for the pan

¾ cup sugar

2 large eggs, beaten, at room temperature

1 teaspoon vanilla extract

Grated zest of 1 lemon

½ cup whole milk

Confectioners' sugar, for sifting

Topping

¾ cup heavy cream

2 tablespoons confectioners' sugar

½ teaspoon vanilla extract

1 To prepare the berries, toss the strawberries and granulated sugar together in a medium bowl. Cover and refrigerate until the berries give off their juices, at least 2 hours or up to 8 hours.

2 Puree 1 cup of the strawberries with their juice and the lemon juice in a blender, adding more granulated sugar to taste. Pour into a sauceboat and cover. Refrigerate the sauce and the remaining strawberries separately until serving.

3 Meanwhile, to make the cake, position a rack in the center of the oven and preheat to 350°F. Lightly butter the inside of a 9-inch round cake pan. Line the bottom of the pan with wax paper. Dust with flour and tap out the excess.

4 Sift the flour, baking powder, and salt together. Beat the butter with an electric mixer on high speed in a medium bowl until smooth. Gradually beat in the granulated sugar and continue beating until light in color and texture, about 3 minutes. Gradually beat in the eggs, then add the vanilla and lemon zest. Add the flour mixture in three additions alternating with the milk in two additions, beating at low speed, scraping down the sides of the bowl as needed, and mixing until just smooth.

5 Spread the batter in the pan. Bake until the cake springs back when lightly pressed in the center with a finger, about 25 minutes. Let cool in the pan on a wire cake rack for 10 minutes. Run a knife around the inside of the pan to loosen the cake. Invert onto the rack and remove the paper. Turn right side up and let cool completely.

6 To make the topping, whip the cream, confectioners' sugar, and vanilla together in a chilled medium bowl with an electric mixer set on high speed until soft peaks form.

7 To serve, transfer the cake to a platter. Sift confectioners' sugar on top. Cut the cake into wedges and place on dessert plates. Top each with equal amounts of the whipped cream and strawberries. Drizzle with the strawberry sauce and serve.

> "I don't feel like I am complacent about anything I've done in the game. I attack each game like I still feel I am hungry, even after thirteen years."

ON THE MENU

CUCUMBER AND TOMATO SALAD
WITH LEMON PEPPER

BIG BATCH MEATBALLS
AND SAUCE

TRIPLE-LAYER CARROT CAKE

PAUL KONERKO

FIRST BASEMAN CHICAGO WHITE SOX

★ When it comes to baseball, even after more than a decade of playing, Chicago White Sox captain Paul Konerko brings his A-game to the field every year. "I show up the same way to play every night, the same way since I was a rookie," says Konerko. As an All-Star and World Series champion, he is a baseball guy through and through.

Konerko, considered one of the finest veterans in the game, is known for his clutch hitting and leadership. And who could forget his killer grand slam during the 2005 World Series, now permanently inked in the baseball record books? How would Konerko describe a World Series championship in one word? "Validating." He says, "It just validated everything about why you always ever played and the way you've gone about it. As a player, you were rewarded for, at least in that one given year, everything you thought about, including how to win and how to play. It all came true in one year."

Back in high school, a shot at the Big Leagues started to look like a reality for Konerko. But if professional baseball hadn't come calling, he and his father had plans for his future education. "I was planning on going to college," he says. "My dad told me if I got drafted and it worked out differently, we'd go from there. But I should plan on getting my education and doing all that first, and if anything else popped up then we'd deal with it." As it turned out, Konerko was a senior in high school when the call from the Big Leagues came, and he was on his way.

After years in the Major Leagues, Konerko knows how to adjust to the game's ups and downs. "It is just like any job in life. I mean, it is not easy and there are a lot of people trying to get in your spot," says Konerko. A professional baseball career begins with physical

"Every Sunday night when I was growing up my mom would make an Italian meal."

skill, he explains, but the climb to the top and holding one's ground is all in the mind. "I think you get drafted and you get into professional baseball based on talent, but how you get through those Minor League seasons and how you get to the Big League and how you stay is definitely a mental thing," he says. "That's part of being a Big Leaguer; it is learning how to deal with all of that stuff."

And having the staying power to be competitive year after year sets Konerko apart from those who came up only for the proverbial "cup of coffee."

"Part of it is, you have to go get it. You have to go out and give it on the field," he explains. "You've got to battle through each year starting from the minor league seasons until now. Even in the great years, it's a battle. I'm definitely fortunate and I feel lucky that I've been in the Big Leagues for over ten years."

Born in Rhode Island, Konerko moved with his family to Arizona when he was eleven years old. Today, he resides in Chicago with his wife and two sons during the season and returns to Arizona, where his extended family still lives, in the off-season. While in Arizona, Konerko continues with mealtime traditions that circle back to his childhood and his Italian heritage. "Every Sunday night when I was growing up my mom would make an Italian meal," he says. Today, his mother's homemade dinner is still a frequent event: "We are pretty much over at my parents' house at least two or three times a month eating an Italian meal together." Veal Parmesan is a favorite, along with pasta and a homemade sauce with meatballs. For dessert, Konerko loves pecan pie and carrot cake. He concedes, "There are not too many things I don't like when it comes to sweets, to be honest."

By his own admission, Konerko is not much of a cook; however, he hopes to learn in the future. Currently, his very short list of culinary skills includes making his favorite snack: "I love cucumbers with olive oil and rice vinegar and lemon pepper. I don't know where I came up with it. I've been eating it for probably fifteen years. I have it three to four times a week. I eat a lot of cucumbers."

With baseball commitments set aside in the winter, Konerko and his wife, Jennifer, enjoy traveling to Napa Valley almost every year. "Right now we are just into drinking different wines and learning about them," he says. And learning to play the guitar is "my number-one thing—to be able to hold down some chords and play in a bar band, that would be kind of cool," he says. "Other than that, I'd like to travel more when I am done playing [baseball]. I definitely want to go to Italy with my wife. That's probably the first trip we'll make."

But for now, Konerko still enjoys making the trip around the bases.

CUCUMBER AND TOMATO SALAD WITH LEMON PEPPER

MAKES 4 SERVINGS

★ Paul Konerko makes this Mediterranean-inspired salad at least once a week, and sometimes up to three times a week. Serve it on its own as a snack, or have fun with it and add your own personalized additions—grilled shrimp or chicken, crumbled feta, and chopped olives are all good.

2 large cucumbers
2 large ripe tomatoes
2 tablespoons extra-virgin olive oil
1½ teaspoons rice vinegar
1 teaspoon lemon pepper
Salt

1 Peel the cucumbers. Cut them in half lengthwise, and use the tip of a teaspoon to scoop out the seeds. Thinly slice the cucumbers and place in a bowl.

2 Core the tomatoes. Cut in half lengthwise and poke out the seeds with your finger. Cut the tomatoes into ½-inch-thick wedges. Add to the bowl.

3 Add the oil, vinegar, and lemon pepper. Season with salt and stir gently to combine. Serve immediately, or cover and refrigerate for up to 1 hour.

BIG BATCH MEATBALLS AND SAUCE

MAKES 4–6 SERVINGS, WITH PLENTY OF LEFTOVER MEATBALLS AND SAUCE

★ Making tomato sauce and meatballs from scratch is a favorite activity for most Italian-American families, including the Konerkos. Start preparing the sauce in the early afternoon, and it will be ready in time for dinner. This version actually comes from my grandmother, but I know the Konerkos would approve. And when it comes to meatball making, roll up your sleeves and make a big batch that will last well beyond Sunday. Extra meatballs can be easily stored in your freezer and reheated for future meals.

Tomato Sauce

4 28-ounce cans crushed tomatoes

1 12-ounce can tomato paste

1 large onion, peeled and left whole

1 tablespoon sugar

1 garlic clove, minced

10 large basil leaves, torn into small pieces

2 tablespoons dried oregano

1 bay leaf

Salt and freshly ground black pepper

Meatballs

3 pounds ground sirloin (90% lean)

2 cups dried Italian-seasoned bread crumbs

1 cup (4 ounces) freshly grated Parmesan

6 large eggs, beaten

2 teaspoons garlic salt

½ teaspoon crushed red pepper flakes

1 tablespoon olive oil, plus more for rolling the meatballs

1 large garlic clove, peeled and crushed

Freshly grated Parmesan, for serving

1 To make the sauce, combine 1 can of cold water with the crushed tomatoes, tomato paste, onion, sugar, garlic, basil, oregano, and bay leaf in a large nonreactive pot. Bring to a boil over high heat. Reduce the heat to low. Simmer, uncovered, stirring occasionally, for 1 hour.

2 Meanwhile, make the meatballs. Combine the ground beef, bread crumbs, Parmesan, eggs, garlic salt, and pepper flakes in a large bowl, and mix well with your hands. Oil your hands to prevent the mixture from sticking, then shape the meat mixture into 45 golf-ball-size meatballs.

3 Heat 1 tablespoon oil and the garlic clove in a large nonstick skillet over medium heat until the garlic is golden but not browned, about 2 minutes. Remove the garlic from the oil with a slotted spoon and discard the garlic. In batches, add the meatballs to the skillet and cook, turning occasionally, until browned on all sides, about 6 minutes. Using the slotted spoon, transfer the meatballs to a platter lined with paper towel to absorb excess oil.

4 Carefully add the meatballs to the sauce and stir gently to submerge them. Simmer, stirring occasionally, until the meatballs are cooked through and the sauce has reduced by about one-fourth, 1½–2 hours longer. Season with salt and pepper.

5 Transfer 1 quart of the sauce to a large serving bowl, discarding the bay leaf when you come across it. Add your favorite cooked pasta and toss well. Serve hot, with the Parmesan passed on the side.

6 Allow the remaining sauce and meatballs to cool. Freeze in airtight containers for up to 3 months.

TRIPLE-LAYER CARROT CAKE

MAKES 12 SERVINGS

★ Gibsons Bar and Steakhouse in Chicago is renowned for its enormous aged steaks and eye-popping desserts. This impressive, towering three-tier carrot cake has made it quite a few fans, including baseball players. At Gibsons, you'll be served a chunk of cake big enough to feed the entire starting lineup, but at home, you might choose to serve smaller slices.

Carrot Cake

Unsalted butter, for the pans

2½ cups all-purpose flour, plus more for the pans

1 tablespoon baking powder

1½ teaspoons ground cinnamon

1 teaspoon salt

3 cups corn oil or vegetable oil

2½ cups sugar

5 large eggs, at room temperature

3 cups (12 ounces) peeled and shredded carrots

2 cups (8 ounces) walnut pieces, toasted and coarsely chopped (see Note)

1⅓ cups large, plump raisins, such as Thompson

Frosting

12 ounces cream cheese, softened at room temperature

9 tablespoons unsalted butter, at room temperature

7½ cups sifted confectioners' sugar

1   To make the cake layers, position racks in the upper third and center of the oven and preheat to 350ºF. Lightly butter the insides of three 9 x 1 ½-inch round cake pans. Line the bottoms of the pans with waxed paper. Dust with flour and tap out the excess.

2   Sift the flour, baking soda, cinnamon, and salt together. Beat the oil, sugar, and eggs in a large bowl with an electric mixer on medium speed until combined. With the mixer on low speed, gradually add in the flour mixture and beat until smooth, scraping

down the sides of the bowl as needed. Add the carrots, walnuts, and raisins, and mix until smooth.

3   Divide the batter evenly among the cake pans and smooth the tops. Bake, spacing the pans well apart without touching, until the batter darkens and the cakes spring back when pressed gently in the centers, about 50 minutes. Let cool in the pans on wire cake racks for 10 minutes. Run a knife around the insides of the pans to loosen the cakes. Invert onto the racks and remove the wax paper. Turn cakes right-side up on the racks and let cool completely.

4   To make the frosting, beat the cream cheese and butter in a large bowl with an electric mixer on high speed, scraping down the sides of the bowl as needed. With the mixer on low speed, gradually beat in the confectioners' sugar. Return the mixer speed to high and beat until light and fluffy, 1–2 minutes.

5   Spoon a dab of the frosting into the center of a cake platter. Place a cake layer, right-side up, on the platter, and spread the top with ⅔ cup of frosting. Top with a second cake layer, and spread the top with another ⅔ cup of frosting. Top with the final layer. Spread the remaining frosting over the top, and then the sides, of the cake. Let the cake stand for at least 1 hour to set the frosting. Slice and serve.

NOTE: To toast the walnuts, spread them on a rimmed baking sheet. Bake in a preheated 350ºF oven, stirring occasionally, until lightly toasted and fragrant, about 10 minutes. Let cool completely before chopping.

> "I try to tell myself to keep it simple as much as I can. This game can get real tough, especially mentally, so I just try to keep it as simple and easy as I can."

EVAN LONGORIA

THIRD BASEMAN TAMPA BAY RAYS

★ As a young, sure-footed player with oodles of talent, Evan Longoria plays the game like a veteran. At the end of his 2008 Major League debut year, Longoria topped off a great season by taking home the American League Rookie of the Year Award. And that same year he helped the Tampa Bay Rays win their first division title and the American League pennant—all at the young age of twenty-two.

Longoria's ascent into the stratosphere of professional baseball began at a somewhat slower pace. Back when he was in high school, Longoria was not sought after by college baseball recruiters. He recalls, "In high school, I didn't get any scholarship offers and I had to go to a junior college where I thought maybe this isn't going to work out and maybe I might have to try a different route." But by the end of Longoria's freshman year at Rio Hondo Community College, he was offered a scholarship to Long Beach State and a flame was ignited: "Once I got to Long Beach I committed myself to trying to make it to the big leagues and I put everything else on the back burner. I basically put all of my energy forward to try and make it." In 2006, the Tampa Bay Rays drafted Longoria in the first round.

But it was only just before Longoria was drafted that he started to believe that he might have a shot at the Major Leagues. During the summer of 2005, Longoria played in the premier collegiate summer baseball league, on Cape Cod. Longoria recalls, "When I played in the Cape Cod League, I played with a bunch of players who were some of the best players in college baseball at the time. They were guys who were looking to get drafted. When I was able to succeed and play well at their level, I started to realize that I might have a chance to do something in this game. Before that, I didn't really think that I could

"Food makes me happy . . . I can really cook anything. I love to cook. I cook all the time, but not as much during the season."

have done it." He adds, "I was excited to go in and be a part of that. I played well in that league. It was a great overall experience." Longoria also had a summer job during his stay on Cape Cod: "I was a camp counselor for a little kids' baseball camp during the day, before my games, and that was cool. I got to meet a bunch of little kids ages seven through twelve years old. I met some good people."

As a born and bred Californian and the eldest of four siblings, Longoria takes it all in stride. He credits his family with having the biggest effect on his baseball career. "First of all, I have a great family. In my opinion, I was raised the right way. Everyone's definition of the right way is different. I think my parents did a tremendous job raising me to be humble and teaching me the right things to do. That definitely helps. There are a lot of distractions and a lot of things that could easily take you off the path, the right path, if you don't watch out," he says.

Longoria's lasting friendships from home also play an important role in his everyday life. "I have a great group of friends . . . two best friends since I was twelve and another best friend since kindergarten," he says. Longoria's baseball schedule doesn't leave him a lot of time to see his friends back in California, but that doesn't stop his childhood pals from getting together in Tampa. A typical night out after a game at Tropicana Field for Longoria and his buddies consists of "a concert, whatever, dinner, or maybe just sitting around and playing video games and telling stories about the past. We play *Rock Band* and *Guitar Hero;* they're all silly, but they are pretty fun. We have a good time."

During the off-season, Longoria catches up with family and friends at his Arizona home. "I love to entertain. I love having people over and to entertain," he says. And the All-Star third baseman professes a strong passion for cooking. Initially taught by his mother and grandmother, whose family heritage is Ukrainian, Longoria also learned about cooking while living as a bachelor. "Food makes me happy," says Longoria. "I like to cook on the grill, you know, the manly-man things like chicken and a slow-cooked rack of ribs, but since I've been living on my own, I've learned other things by just looking up a recipe and giving it a try. I can really cook anything. I love to cook. I cook all the time, but not as much during the season."

Longoria considers his mother's stuffed cabbage and potato dumplings, two popular Ukrainian specialties, his favorite home-cooked dishes, but notes that his grandfather's homemade vegetable soup "with a nice grilled cheese" is at the top of his list, too. And as for desserts, Longoria claims, "I'm not much of a dessert maker, but I do love eating desserts. My grandpa makes awesome pies. I've always loved his apple pies, but he is known in our family for his classic lemon meringue pie."

During the off-season, Longoria catches up on movies, plays golf, and works on teaching himself to play the drums. "I just bought a drum set. One of the guys back at the field had a drum set and I just started messing around with it, so I went and got one of my own," he says. At the end of the day, Longoria is just another ordinary twenty-something who happens to have some serious baseball talent.

UKRAINIAN VEGETABLE SOUP

MAKES 8 SERVINGS

★ In honor of Evan Longoria's grandfather's vegetable soup, this version is filled with Eastern European flavors like dill and cabbage. Try to make it with homemade beef broth, if possible, though store-bought broth is acceptable too. Just be sure to buy the reduced-sodium kind.

2 tablespoons vegetable oil

1 large yellow onion, chopped

2 medium carrots, cut into ¼-inch-thick rounds

2 medium celery ribs, cut into ¼-inch-thick slices

1 large baking potato, peeled and cut into ¾-inch cubes

2 garlic cloves, minced

2 quarts beef broth, preferably homemade (or use canned reduced-sodium beef broth)

3 cups coarsely chopped green cabbage

5 fresh ripe tomatoes or drained canned plum tomatoes, coarsely chopped

½ teaspoon dried thyme

1 bay leaf

2 tablespoons chopped fresh dill, plus more for serving

Salt and freshly ground black pepper

Sour cream for serving

1   Heat the oil in a large soup pot over medium heat. Add the onion, carrots, celery, potato, and garlic and cover. Cook, stirring occasionally, until the onions are tender, about 5 minutes. Add the broth, cabbage, tomatoes, thyme, and bay leaf and bring to a boil over high heat. Reduce the heat to medium-low and simmer until the vegetables are tender, about 1 hour.

2   Stir in the dill and season with salt and pepper. Simmer for 10 minutes more. Remove the bay leaf. Serve the soup hot, garnished with a dollop of sour cream and additional dill.

STUFFED CABBAGE (HOLUBTSI)

MAKES 8 SERVINGS

★ This great Ukrainian delicacy was a standard in Longoria's childhood home. Stuffed cabbage is still at the top of Evan's list, especially when made by his mother, Ellie, from a family recipe. I adapted it just a bit by adding raisins and brown sugar for sweetness.

1 large green cabbage, cored

⅓ cup long-grain rice

1 pound ground round (85% lean)

1 medium onion, finely chopped

½ cup golden raisins

1 teaspoon salt

½ teaspoon freshly ground black pepper

2 10-ounce cans tomato soup

2 tablespoons light brown sugar

1 Position a rack in the center of the oven and preheat to 375ºF. Lightly oil a 15 x 10-inch baking dish.

2 Bring a large pot of water to a boil over high heat. Add the cabbage and cook, removing each leaf with two wooden spoons as it softens and separates from the head. Transfer the cabbage leaves to a bowl of cold water. You need 16 whole cabbage leaves. (Save the remaining cabbage for another use.) Using a sharp knife, shave the thick stem of each leaf to make it easier to roll up the filled cabbage leaf.

3 Meanwhile, bring a medium saucepan of lightly salted water to a boil over high heat. Add the rice and cook it, just like pasta, until tender, about 20 minutes. Drain in a wire sieve and rinse under cold water. Set aside.

4 Combine the ground round, onion, raisins, rice, salt, and pepper in a medium bowl. Place a cabbage leaf on the work surface. Place about ¼ cup of the ground round mixture in a strip on the lower third of the leaf. Fold in the sides, then roll up the leaf from the bottom. Place seam side down in the baking dish. Continue with the remaining leaves and ground round mixture.

5 Whisk the soup and 2½ cups water together. Pour over the cabbage and sprinkle with the brown sugar. Cover the dish with a lightly oiled sheet of aluminum foil (oiled side down), making sure the foil doesn't touch the cabbage leaves.

6 Bake until the cabbage is very tender, about 1½ hours. Let stand for 10 minutes, then serve hot.

POTATO DUMPLINGS

MAKES ABOUT 6 DOZEN DUMPLINGS, 8–10 SERVINGS

★ Ukrainians call these delectable dumplings *vareniki,* but you may know them in their Polish incarnation, pierogi. No matter what you call them, they are labor-intensive but worth every second of effort. Many families gather the forces together to fold a mountain of dumplings for holidays. The Longorias serve them boiled, but you can also fry the cooked dumplings in butter until they are golden brown. In either case, they are always topped with sour cream and sautéed onions.

Filling

3 large baking potatoes (2 pounds), such as russet or Burbank, scrubbed but not peeled

2 cups (8 ounces) shredded cheddar

Salt and freshly ground black pepper

Dough

4 cups all-purpose flour, plus more for kneading and for the baking sheet

8 tablespoons (1 stick) unsalted butter, at room temperature, cut into tablespoons

1 cup warm water

2 large eggs, beaten

Assembly

2 tablespoons unsalted butter

2 large yellow onions, chopped

Salt and freshly ground black pepper

Sour cream, for serving

1 To make the filling, put the potatoes in a large saucepan and add enough lightly salted cold water to cover. Cover the saucepan and bring to a boil over high heat. Reduce the heat to low and simmer, with the lid ajar, until the potatoes are tender, about 30 minutes. Drain and rinse under cold water. Let cool until easy to handle. Peel and mash the potatoes well. Stir in the cheddar. Season with salt and pepper.

2 To make the dough, combine the flour and butter in a large bowl. Using your fingertips, rub the butter into the flour until the mixture is crumbly. Make a well in the center and add the warm water and eggs. Mix with your hands to make a soft dough. Transfer to a floured work surface and knead, adding more flour as needed, until the dough is smooth, about 3 minutes. Cover with a clean kitchen towel and let stand for 10 minutes.

3 Cut the dough into quarters. Dust two rimmed baking sheets with flour. Work with one quarter at a time, keeping the remaining dough covered with the towel. Dust the top of the dough with flour and roll out into a 13- to 14-inch round about 1/16 inch thick. Using a 3½-inch diameter round cookie cutter or an inverted glass, cut out rounds of dough. Reserve the trimmings in a plastic bag. Working with one dough round at a time, moisten the edges of the round with water. Place a scant teaspoon of filling in the bottom half of the round. Fold the round in half and pinch the edges completely closed. Transfer to a floured baking sheet. Repeat with the remaining rounds, being sure that the dumplings do not touch one another. Continue with the remaining dough and filling, adding the trimmings to the plastic bag. Knead the trimmings together, then let stand for 10 minutes. Roll out the trimmings to make the final batch of rounds. (Do not try to roll out any subsequent trimmings, as they will be too tough.) The dumplings can be formed, loosely covered, and refrigerated for up to 4 hours.

4 When you're ready to serve the dumplings, melt the butter in a large skillet over medium heat. Add the onions and cook, stirring often, until golden brown, about 10 minutes. Season with salt and pepper. Reduce the heat to very low and cover the skillet to keep the onions warm.

5 Bring a large pot of lightly salted water to a boil over high heat. In 2 or 3 batches, add the dumplings and cook until tender, about 3 minutes. Using a wire spider or a sieve, lift the dumplings out of the water, transfer them to a bowl, and cover the bowl with a kitchen towel to keep warm.

6 Serve the dumplings in bowls, topped with a dollop of sour cream and a spoonful of onions.

"Do what makes you happy. You know, there are a lot of people out there that are doing things they don't enjoy. Just try to do what makes you happy."

JOE MAUER

CATCHER MINNESOTA TWINS

★ Since his 2004 Major League debut, Joe Mauer has played for the Minnesota Twins, a team whose ballpark is just up the road from his childhood home. "Well, ever since I was younger, five or six years old, I always wanted to play in the Big Leagues," he says, "and growing up in Minnesota I always watched the Twins—Kent Hrbek and Kirby Puckett. I got a little older and some other things came into play, but it was always baseball for me."

Born and raised in St. Paul, Mauer is already a four-time All-Star and the recipient of numerous Gold Glove, Silver Slugger, and batting champion awards, as well as an MVP title. In 2006, he became the first American League catcher *ever* to win a batting title, and the first catcher in the Majors to win a batting title since 1942. Mauer is a phenomenal player who gives new meaning to the phrase "home-field advantage." With an unassuming personality and a good-hearted nature, he is baseball's All-American homegrown hero.

The youngest of three boys, Mauer is very close to his brothers, his parents, and his grandparents. His entire family can often be seen rooting for Mauer at his home games. "My mom's parents have only missed four or five of my home games. And I am now in my seventh season," says Mauer. He adds, "Baseball was always one of my favorite things to do as a family." Mauer often credits his family for keeping him grounded: "Well, family will do that. If you were to meet my family, you'd see why." And he often teases his father about the source of his athletic ability, claiming that it was his mother, a grade-school gym teacher, from whom he inherited his athletic skills. Mauer says with a slight smile, "It all comes from my mom, and my dad doesn't like that too much, but I think it did definitely come from my mom."

"I try to eat as healthily as I can when I am in season, but often I just try and grab any food I can and keep my weight up."

When it comes to a home-cooked meal, Mauer is quick to say, "Mom's lasagna is number one. It's definitely simple, but I think because it comes from Mom it means a little bit more." Before he achieved Major League stardom, Mauer started his Minor League years alongside his older brother Jake. His mother's lasagna was a treat after a long day in single-A ball. Mauer fondly recalls, "When I was playing in the Minor Leagues, you know, one of my first stops was in Quad Cities, Iowa—a five-hour drive from where I grew up, and one of my mother's things was to visit me and my brother and bring along a home-made pan of lasagna. She'd make a pan [of lasagna] quite a bit when we were younger. She still does."

Mauer maintains a friendship with fellow teammate Justin Morneau. "Probably my best friend in baseball is Justin Morneau," says Mauer. It was during one of their winning streaks that Mauer, on a whim, decided to join Morneau in one of his food rituals at the local sandwich shop. According to Mauer, Morneau is very superstitious. "Back in 2006, we had a great year," recalls Mauer. "I won the batting title and he won the MVP. I remember during one home stand we went to our local sandwich shop before our game. Later that night we won, so we went back the next day and had another good night of baseball, won that night, and so on. We ended up eating the same sandwich—mine was a turkey sub— at the same sandwich shop for seven days in a row. I did this to amuse him, but maybe it was his superstition rubbing off on me." Years later, a turkey club is still Mauer's favorite sandwich.

During the baseball season Mauer likes to eat healthy foods, including edamame as a between-meals snack. Given his intense workouts, though, he says, "I try to eat as healthily as I can when I am in season, but often I just try and grab any food I can and keep my weight up." His favorite two desserts—which will definitely help keep his weight up—are cheesecake and chocolate cake. "I like cheesecake, but it's got to be plain New York–style cheesecake with maybe a little sauce on it—raspberry sauce on it. If you have a chocolate cake with fudge, hot fudge, and ice cream on it, I'm all over it." And as for crullers: "I've been known to crush a few of those every now and then." Though not much of a kitchen maven, Mauer does grill occasionally. "I marinate a chicken breast with Italian dressing and cook it on the grill," he says. And as a definitive bachelor, Mauer admits to eating many meals in front of his TV while outstretched on his black leather sofa. "I like to start my day by watching the MLB channel so I can catch up on all the highlights from games the night before," he says. But make no mistake; Mauer is no couch potato. This superstar athlete—arguably the best catcher in the game—is in top form. Mauer even practices yoga in the off-season to help increase his flexibility in the catcher's crouch. He started

yoga with former teammate Jason Bartlett. "We figured we'd try it out by watching a DVD at home rather than going to a club and embarrassing ourselves," he says.

Whether in a warrior pose, behind the dish, or up to bat, Mauer is one of Minnesota's finest athletes.

TURKEY CLUB WRAP WITH EDAMAME HUMMUS

MAKES 2 SERVINGS

★ I created this great lunch to combine two of Joe's favorite foods, a turkey club sandwich and edamame. The result is a light but filling wrap that uses a flavorful edamame hummus in place of mayonnaise. Keep the hummus in mind when you want something fresh-tasting to serve with vegetables or crackers as a dip, too. Many supermarkets now carry frozen shelled edamame, and you are sure to find them at your local natural foods market.

Edamame Hummus

1 cup frozen shelled edamame, thawed

2 tablespoons freshly squeezed lemon juice

Pinch of cayenne pepper

¼ cup extra-virgin olive oil

Salt and freshly ground black pepper

Wrap

2 9-inch whole wheat tortillas

4 large red-leaf lettuce leaves, washed and dried

4 ounces thinly sliced cooked turkey

4 slices cooked turkey bacon or pork bacon

1 ripe plum tomato, seeded and diced

1 To make the edamame hummus, puree the edamame, lemon juice, and cayenne in a food processor. With the machine running, gradually add the oil through the feed tube, and process until smooth. Season with salt and pepper. Transfer the hummus to a bowl.

2 For each wrap, spread half of the hummus over a tortilla, leaving a 1-inch border around the edges. Top with 2 lettuce leaves, overlapping as needed, then half of the turkey and 2 bacon slices. Sprinkle with half of the diced tomato. Fold in the right and left sides of the tortilla about 2 inches, then tightly roll up from the bottom. Cut wrap in half crosswise, transfer to a plate, and serve.

ALL-AMERICAN LASAGNA

MAKES 8–12 SERVINGS

★ Teresa Mauer always made two pans of her lasagna for her son Joe, one to eat immediately and one to freeze for a later meal. This lasagna touches all of the bases with everything that makes lasagna a hit with hungry sons (and the moms who love them) everywhere. It's not authentically Italian, but when it is this good . . . who cares?

Meat Sauce

2 tablespoons olive oil

1 large onion, chopped

3 garlic cloves, minced

2 pounds ground round (85% lean)

1 28-ounce can crushed tomatoes

1 6-ounce can tomato paste

2 teaspoons dried oregano

2 teaspoons dried basil

1 bay leaf

Salt and freshly ground black pepper

Lasagna

1 pound lasagna noodles

1 32-ounce container small-curd cottage cheese or ricotta cheese

2 large eggs, beaten

3 cups (12 ounces) shredded mozzarella

1½ cups (6 ounces) freshly grated Parmesan

1 To make the sauce, heat the oil in a large saucepan over medium heat. Add the onion and cook, stirring often, until softened, about 3 minutes. Add the garlic and cook until fragrant, about 1 minute. Add the ground round and cook, stirring often to break up the meat with the sides of the spoon, until it loses its raw look, about 8 minutes. Drain off the fat from the saucepan.

2 Stir in the crushed tomatoes, tomato paste, 2 cups water, the oregano, the basil, and the bay leaf and bring to a simmer. Reduce the heat to medium-low and simmer, uncovered, until slightly thickened and reduced to about 2 quarts, about 30 minutes. Discard the bay leaf. Season with salt and pepper.

3 Position a rack in the center of the oven and preheat the oven to 350°F. Lightly oil a 15 x 10-inch baking dish.

4 Bring a large pot of lightly salted water to a boil over high heat. Add the noodles and cook, following the package directions, until al dente. Drain and rinse under cold water. Spread the noodles on kitchen towels and pat dry. You will have extra noodles, which allows for broken ones.

5 Mix the cottage cheese and eggs together in a bowl. Spread about ½ cup of the meat sauce in the bottom of the baking dish. Place 5 noodles in the dish (4 horizontally and 1 vertically), trimming to fit the dish. Top with one-third of the meat sauce, half of the cottage cheese mixture, half of the shredded mozzarella, and ½ cup of the Parmesan. Repeat with 5 more noodles, another third of the meat sauce, the remaining cottage cheese, the remaining mozzarella, and ½ cup of Parmesan. Top with 5 more noodles, the remaining meat sauce, and the remaining Parmesan cheese. Cover with a sheet of lightly oiled aluminum foil, oiled side down.

6 Bake for 35 minutes. Uncover and continue baking until the lasagna is bubbling and heated through, about 35 minutes more. Let stand for 10 minutes before cutting. Serve hot.

NEW YORK CHEESECAKE WITH RASPBERRY SAUCE

MAKES 12 SERVINGS

★ Joe Mauer would love my mom's cheesecake, as it is exactly the way he prefers his—simple, traditional, and something that any New York delicatessen would serve with pride. It stands tall, dense, and creamy on a graham cracker crust, and it is served with a fresh raspberry sauce that cuts through its richness. The cream cheese must be really soft, so let it stand at room temperature a couple of hours before mixing the batter; overnight is not too long.

Cheesecake

1 cup graham cracker crumbs

2 tablespoons unsalted butter, melted

2 pounds cream cheese, at room temperature

1¾ cups plus 2 teaspoons sugar

4 large eggs, at room temperature, beaten

½ teaspoon almond extract

½ teaspoon vanilla extract

1¼ cups sour cream

Raspberry Sauce

2 6-ounce containers fresh raspberries

2 tablespoons sugar

1 teaspoon freshly squeezed lemon juice

1 Position a rack in the center of the oven and pre-heat to 350°F. Lightly butter a 9-inch springform pan.

2 To make the cheesecake, mix the cracker crumbs and melted butter together in a small bowl. Press firmly and evenly into the bottom of the pan.

3 Beat the cream cheese with an electric mixer set on high speed until smooth. Gradually beat in 1¾ cups sugar, then the eggs. Beat in the almond and vanilla extracts. Pour into the pan and smooth the top.

4 Bake until the edges have risen but the very center seems barely set when the pan is gently shaken, about 55 minutes. Remove from the oven. Whisk the sour cream and the remaining 2 teaspoons sugar together. Spread evenly over the top of the cheesecake. Return to the oven and bake until the topping looks set, about 10 minutes.

5 Remove cake from the oven and let stand for 2 minutes. Run a sharp knife around the inside of the pan. Return the cake to the turned-off oven. Let cool completely in the oven.

6 Remove the sides of the pan. Wrap the cheesecake in plastic wrap and refrigerate until chilled, at least 4 hours or overnight.

7 To make the raspberry sauce, puree the raspberries, sugar, and lemon juice in a blender or food processor until smooth. Strain through a fine wire sieve to remove the seeds. Pour into a sauceboat.

8 Cut the cheesecake with a thin knife dipped into hot water before each slice. Serve chilled, with the raspberry sauce.

> "I'm not very big, but I play baseball as hard as I can. I hope I can be a good role model to kids."

DUSTIN PEDROIA

SECOND BASEMAN BOSTON RED SOX

★ Dustin Pedroia is anything but your typical-looking Major Leaguer. At well under six feet tall and a trim 165 pounds, he doesn't look the part. "No one really notices me walking down the street," admits Pedroia. "I look like a normal guy." But don't be deceived by looks. Beneath the surface, Pedroia has a million kilowatts of energy, and he is often at the forefront of the action on the diamond. Within the first two years of his Major League career, Pedroia was Rookie of the Year, American League MVP, an All-Star, a Silver Slugger, a Gold Glove recipient, and—most important for Red Sox fans—a key player in the team's successful quest to win the 2007 World Series.

Though not one to dwell on the downside of things, Pedroia acknowledges that his career in the Big Leagues got off to a rocky start. He had to work hard to earn his spot as the Red Sox starting second baseman: "When I first got called up, I really struggled, but I am most proud of just fighting through that and proving everybody wrong and being successful. I don't think anybody thought I could do it—be a good Major League player, let alone accomplish some of the things I have done." He adds, "I started playing baseball when I was a little kid and I always loved it. I thought it was fun. I never really thought that I would ever be a professional. I'm not very big, you know." Pedroia may not be of great size for a professional athlete, but to Red Sox Nation he is undeniably big, *wicked big*.

These days, hanging out with his Major League teammates continues to be enjoyable for Pedroia. "Just being around the guys, being around your teammates. That's a lot of fun. You build relationships with guys who are from every different kind of background, different countries, and you're on one team and you're trying to do one thing and that's

"I'll have pasta, steak, chicken, or fish . . . And I'll eat any vegetable—I'm not a picky eater."

win," says Pedroia. And for Pedroia, who is the energizer of his team, winning involves "just working hard and always staying up on my weightlifting program, always hitting, always taking ground balls, always watching video, and that's the only way you can do it. Don't get too up or down; you've got to get out there and stay on your game."

Keeping on top of his game hasn't always been easy. In 2006, he was a Major League athlete, but he admits he wasn't exactly in top form. "I was kind of chunky," he whispers. "I didn't know how to eat. I would get home and crush anything. And my energy was down sometimes." Pedroia knew he needed to make a change in his diet and fitness routine. After consulting a nutritional expert during the 2007 off-season, Pedroia worked hard to improve his eating habits. "Now, I feel great," proclaims the super-fit Pedroia.

Though Pedroia's healthy eating is a big part of his daily routine, he admits to keeping a balance by indulging in guilt-free eating once a week. He says with a grin, "Every Wednesday during the off-season, Andre Ethier and I go to a Mexican restaurant that is about two miles from our homes. I think that one day a week is kind of like a free day for eating, but I do it with only one meal. I probably throw down about 3,000 calories. So that's it. I will eat some tacos, rice and beans, an enchilada, and probably two bags of chips and salsa." And during the season, Pedroia admits to having one pregame routine. He says, "I drink chocolate milk every time, right before a game, at 6 p.m.—right before I shower and get ready. It kind of sticks to you and fills you up a little bit."

Pedroia's high-octane nature doesn't wane even in the off-season. "I took four days off after last year," he concedes. "I am a big believer in 'never get out of shape' because it is so hard to get back into shape. If I took a month off in November, it would take me all of December to get back to where I was. And I don't want that. I want to make sure I am gaining and not maintaining." Whether during the season or not, Pedroia starts his day with a healthy breakfast. "I usually have three scrambled eggs, two pieces of wheat toast (I don't like butter; I like marmalade jelly), and an orange or berries, either strawberries or blueberries or something like that. And I usually eat that every morning—every single day, even on the road. It's just kind of a routine and I never get sick of it," he says. Throughout the day, Pedroia makes sure he has protein to keep his energy high. Before lunch he will have either a blended shake with mixed berries or a snack of fruit with peanut butter. "I'll have an apple with peanut butter or a banana with peanut butter or a peanut butter and banana sandwich on wheat toast," he says.

For lunch, Pedroia does not like sandwiches. "I'll have pasta or steak, chicken or fish. I like all seafood, from salmon to oysters to shrimp. And I'll eat any vegetable—I'm not a picky eater. But I hate brussels sprouts," he says.

Raised in California, Pedroia recognizes his mother for teaching him a few things about cooking, including how to make homemade pasta sauces. At home, he says, "I make all kinds of pasta sauces." And as a new parent himself, Pedroia enjoys spending time with his wife, Kelli, and their toddler son, Dylan. About his son, Pedroia proudly declares, "He's awesome. He has a lot of energy." Like father, like son.

LOW AND SLOW SCRAMBLED EGGS

MAKES 1–2 SERVINGS

★ Scrambled eggs are a snap, as long as you don't rush them. High heat causes rubbery scrambled eggs, so keep the heat low and steady. Dustin Pedroia likes his eggs very plain, with just salt and pepper (extra pepper, please). Serve your breakfast Pedroia-style with two slices of wheat toast topped with marmalade and a side of fresh fruit, such as mixed berries or a juicy orange.

3 large eggs
¼ teaspoon salt
Freshly ground black pepper
½ teaspoon olive oil

1 Beat the eggs in a bowl with the salt and as much pepper as you like until they are foamy.

2 Heat the oil in a nonstick medium skillet over medium-low heat. When the skillet is warm, add the eggs. Cook until the eggs are set around the edges, about 1 minute. Using a heatproof spatula, stir and fold the eggs over on themselves. Continue cooking, stirring and folding every 15 seconds or so, until the eggs are set and bright yellow. Serve hot.

PASTA PRIMAVERA

MAKES 4–6 SERVINGS

★ Pasta primavera is a vegetable-packed Italian staple, but it is often overloaded with cream, which can offset the healthful qualities of the vegetables. This version, designed with Dustin Pedroia's sensible eating habits (and his passion for pasta) in mind, is low in fat but high in flavor. Another plus is that the sauce comes together in about the same time it takes for the pasta to cook.

1 pound dried fettuccine
2 teaspoons extra-virgin olive oil
2 tablespoons finely chopped shallots
1 garlic clove, minced
1 pound asparagus, woody stems discarded, cut into 1-inch pieces
1 pound cherry tomatoes, cut in half
1 cup canned reduced-sodium chicken broth
1 teaspoon tomato paste
¼ cup chopped fresh basil
Salt and freshly ground black pepper
Freshly grated Parmesan cheese, for serving

1 Bring a large pot of lightly salted water to a boil over high heat. Add the fettuccine and cook, according to the package directions, until al dente.

2 Meanwhile, heat the oil, shallots, and garlic in a nonstick large skillet over medium heat, stirring often, until softened, about 2 minutes. Add the asparagus and ¼ cup water and cover. Cook until the asparagus turns bright green, about 1 minute. Uncover and add the tomatoes, broth, and tomato paste. Cook, stirring often, until the tomatoes wilt, about 3 minutes. Stir in the basil and season with salt and pepper.

3 Drain the fettuccine and return to the cooking pot. Add the vegetable mixture and stir well. Serve in bowls, sprinkling each serving with 1 tablespoon of Parmesan, with the extra Parmesan passed on the side.

GREEN APPLES WITH MACADAMIA BUTTER

MAKES 2 SERVINGS

⭐ Peanut butter is terrific, but explore other nut butters, such as almond butter and cashew butter, as alternatives. Dustin Pedroia loves macadamia nuts, so macadamia butter adds another delicious dimension to a super-quick snack here.

½ cup macadamia nut butter, or as needed
2 Granny Smith apples, cored and cut into quarters

Spread about 1 tablespoon of macadamia nut butter on each apple quarter, or as much or as little as you like. Eat immediately.

BERRY PROTEIN SMOOTHIE

MAKES 1 GENEROUS SERVING

⭐ For a protein lift during the day, Pedroia relies on a thirst-quenching fruit smoothie. To make a quick, easy and nourishing drink whenever the mood strikes, keep bags of fruit in the freezer. Commercially frozen fruit is very reliable and captures produce at the peak of its flavor. This basic recipe should serve as a blueprint for your own creations.

1 cup whole or skim milk
1 ripe banana, sliced
¾ cup frozen berries, such as blueberries, raspberries, strawberries, or a combination
3 tablespoons protein powder, preferably vanilla

Combine the milk, banana, berries, and protein powder in a blender. Process until smooth. Pour into a tall glass and serve immediately.

"Sometimes I tell myself, wow! And I pinch myself and I wonder if this is a dream. As a poor young little boy growing up . . . I never thought this would happen . . . I never thought I would be so successful."

ON THE MENU
HOME RUN CHICKEN
DOMINICAN BEANS AND RICE
CRÈME BRÛLÉE

ALBERT PUJOLS

FIRST BASEMAN ST. LOUIS CARDINALS

★ As a child growing up in the Dominican Republic, Albert Pujols loved to play baseball. Raised by his grandmother in Santo Domingo, Pujols explains, "in the Dominican [it] is pretty much what you do, you just play the sport all year long."

Without the means to buy their own baseball equipment, Pujols and friends would share among themselves, he explains: "I used to share a glove and spikes with a friend the day that he didn't play." And once Pujols did get his very own baseball gear, he learned his first lesson the hard way. "I was around ten or eleven years old before I owned a bat or a glove," he remembers. "And when I did, somebody stole it from me from the back of my backpack. I was pretty upset."

That was nearly twenty years ago, and since then, Pujols has come a long way. Revered and respected by everyone in the game, the All-Star first baseman for the St. Louis Cardinals is one of the greatest players in baseball. He is a winner because of his phenomenal hitting, which includes driving in a minimum of one hundred RBIs for ten consecutive years. Not to mention hitting over .300 and bashing more than thirty home runs in every season of his career, as well as his long list of individual accomplishments and team championships, including a 2006 World Series victory.

Making his residence in St. Louis with his wife, Deidre, and their four young children, Pujols prefers the comforts of home when he is not playing baseball. "When I am home, I don't go out," he says. "I watch TV, but I don't like to watch sports in the off-season. I take a break from sports and everything." To stay in shape in the off-season, Pujols trains hard.

"Every time I go to Miami, I eat at my grandmother's house."

"I have a routine. I take the whole month of November off and start working out as of December. I go to the gym, lift weights, and do cardio," he says. Pujols reveals that the cardio portion of his workout is his least favorite exercise, even though he dedicates one and a half hours of his day to it—for three and a half months of the off-season, six days a week, until he reports to Spring Training. "Cardio is the hardest part, but it's something you need to do to stay in shape," he concedes.

When Pujols relaxes at home, he prefers to watch suspense thrillers and is an avid fan of TV programs such as *24* and *Prison Break*. "I am the guy who waits until it is all done and I buy the DVD and watch every episode at once," he says. "I like watching movies and spending quality time with my kids." Under the influence of his two daughters, Isabella and Sophia, Pujols surprises himself by being somewhat well versed on the popular animated program *Dora the Explorer*. "Our two dogs are named after the characters Dora and Diego," he admits.

Though far from his early days back in the Dominican Republic, Pujols remains close to his roots, especially when it comes to home cooking. His favorite meal is always the traditional food that his grandmother cooked for him as a kid. Since she now lives in Florida, Pujols still gets to enjoy a taste of home when he visits her. "Every time I go to Miami, I eat at my grandmother's house," says Pujols. And his grandmother taught Pujols's wife, Deidre, her secrets to cooking delicious Dominican meals. Today, Pujols enjoys Deidre's cooking just as much as his grandmother's. "I love rice, chicken, and beans every day. I know how to make rice, too," he says proudly. Among his list of favorite meals, when eating at home, are empanadas, tostones, and pineapple upside-down cake. "My wife makes a great, great pineapple upside-down cake," he says. But when it comes to dessert, Pujols ranks crème brûlée as his first choice.

When it is close to game time, Pujols prefers to eat ligher fare. "Before a game, I don't like to get too full. Around 6:30 p.m., right before the game, I like to eat strawberries, grapes, raspberries, and blackberries in a jug, and mix it together with granola. I like that as a pregame snack," he says.

Deidre has mastered a signature chicken dish for her husband, appropriately named Home Run Chicken. When the Cardinals are in town, she often makes enough for her husband, his Latino teammates, and sometimes even players from the visiting team. "In St. Louis, nothing is better than having your own flavors from home," says Pujols. "It tastes great. I love it." But watch out opposing teams. When Pujols eats Home Run Chicken before a game, he is likely to knock one out of the park.

Pujols is also a winner off the field. Giving back to the community and having a very strong faith are two subjects close to his heart. "God has given me more than what I really

deserve. It's been an amazing ride and amazing career every day, but I thank God every day," says Pujols. To give back, Pujols and his wife established, and are actively involved in, the Pujols Family Foundation, a charity that seeks to improve the lives of the less fortunate, including families from the underprivileged Dominican neighborhoods he knew as a child. "I don't want to be remembered as a great athlete," says Pujols. "Off the field, that is how I want people to remember me. That's really what it is all about."

HOME RUN CHICKEN

MAKES 4 SERVINGS

★ Deidre Pujols is one of those lucky people who seem to be natural-born cooks, although she gives a lot of the credit for her best Dominican recipes to her husband Albert's grandmother, America. She dubbed this braised poultry main course, which sings outs with zesty Latino flavors, Home Run Chicken. It is a home run in my book, for sure.

½ cup chopped yellow onion

½ cup seeded and chopped green bell pepper

¼ cup seeded and chopped red bell pepper

4 sprigs fresh cilantro

2 garlic cloves, crushed under a knife and peeled

½ teaspoon dried oregano

⅓ cup distilled white vinegar

2 tablespoons vegetable oil

Pinch sugar

1 3½-pound chicken, cut up, skin removed from all pieces except the wings

2 chicken bouillon cubes, crushed

1 teaspoon tomato paste

1 teaspoon ground cumin

Salt and freshly ground black pepper

1　Combine the onion, green pepper, red pepper, cilantro, garlic, oregano, and vinegar in a blender and pulse until the vegetables are very finely chopped. Set aside.

2　Heat the oil and sugar in a Dutch oven or flame-proof casserole over medium heat until the sugar melts and begins to caramelize. Add the chicken and cook, turning occasionally, until browned on all sides, about 10 minutes. Transfer the chicken to a plate.

3　Add 1 cup water, the onion mixture, bouillon, tomato paste, and cumin. Bring to a boil, stirring up the browned bits in the pan with a wooden spoon. Return the chicken and any juices on the plate to the Dutch oven. Add enough water to barely cover the chicken and bring to a boil. Reduce the heat to medium-low. Cook at a brisk simmer, uncovered, turning the chicken occasionally, until the chicken is cooked through, about 45 minutes. Transfer the chicken to a deep serving platter and tent with aluminum foil to keep warm.

4　Increase the heat to high. Boil, stirring often, until the cooking liquid is reduced by one-fourth, about 5 minutes. Season with salt and pepper, although you may not need much because of the salty bouillon. Pour over the chicken and serve hot.

DOMINICAN BEANS AND RICE

MAKES 6 SERVINGS

★ Beans and rice are the ultimate Latino side dishes, served alongside everything from grilled chicken to roast pork. This Pujols family recipe for saucy beans is tastier than most, with two kinds of pork and diced winter squash lending flavor to what could be a commonplace dish. And if you've ever wondered why rice tastes better at Latino restaurants, there is a reason: Medium-grain rice, found in the Latino or rice section of the market, is starchier than typical long-grain rice.

Red Beans

1 tablespoon olive oil

1 slice of bacon, coarsely chopped

1 2-ounce link of smoked chorizo sausage, chopped

¼ cup chopped yellow onion

¼ cup seeded and chopped green bell pepper

¼ cup (¼-inch dice) peeled calabaza (Latino pumpkin) or butternut squash

1 tablespoon tomato paste

2 garlic cloves, minced

1 chicken bouillon cube, crushed

2 19-ounce cans of small red beans, drained and rinsed

Rice

1 tablespoon olive oil

1 teaspoon salt

1½ cups medium-grain rice

1 To make the beans, heat the oil in a medium saucepan over medium heat. Add the bacon and cook, stirring occasionally, until lightly browned, about 5 minutes.

2 Stir in 1½ cups water, the chorizo, onion, green pepper, squash, tomato paste, garlic, and bouillon. Bring to a boil, reduce the heat to medium-low, and simmer for 10 minutes. Stir in the beans and cook until heated through, about 10 minutes.

3 To make the rice, bring 3 cups water to a boil with the oil and salt in a medium saucepan over high heat. Add the rice and stir. Reduce the heat to low and cover tightly. Cover until the rice is tender and has absorbed the water, about 20 minutes. Remove from the heat and let stand, covered, for 5 minutes.

4 Fluff the rice with a fork. Serve the rice and beans together or separately.

CRÈME BRÛLÉE

MAKES 6 SERVINGS

★ Crème brûlée, a rich custard with "burnt" sugar on top, sounds daunting to make, but it is actually quite simple and has only a few ingredients. Albert Pujols likes to stay in shape, but this is the one dessert he finds hard to resist. You will need a handheld butane kitchen torch and six ¾-cup (6-ounce) ramekins for this recipe.

2¾ cups heavy cream
⅓ cup plus 1 tablespoon sugar
1 vanilla bean or 1 teaspoon vanilla extract
6 large egg yolks
3 tablespoons sugar, for topping

1 Position a rack in the center of the oven and preheat to 300°F.

2 Combine the cream and sugar in a medium, heavy-bottomed saucepan. If using, split the vanilla bean lengthwise and scrape the seeds into the saucepan with the tip of a knife. Add the bean halves to the saucepan. Bring to a simmer, stirring occasionally. Remove from the heat. Discard the vanilla bean halves. (If using vanilla extract, stir it in now.)

3 Whisk the egg yolks in a medium bowl. Gradually whisk in the hot cream mixture. Strain through a wire sieve into a 1-quart glass measuring cup or pitcher. Divide the custard evenly among six ¾-cup (6-ounce) ramekins or crème brûlée dishes.

4 Arrange the ramekins in a shallow roasting pan. Place the pan on the oven rack. Gently slide the rack out of the oven and add enough hot water to come about halfway up the sides of the ramekins. Carefully slide the rack with the pan back into the oven. Bake until the custards are barely set (the custard will move as a unit when the pan is shaken, but the very center will seem slightly unset), about 40 minutes (or 25 minutes if using crème brûlée dishes). Do not overcook. Remove the pan from the oven. Using tongs, transfer the ramekins to a wire cake rack and let cool.

5 Cover each ramekin with plastic wrap and refrigerate until chilled, at least 3 hours or up to 2 days.

6 Just before serving, uncover the ramekins. Sprinkle 1½ teaspoons sugar evenly over the top of each custard. Using a kitchen torch, held so the flame touches the sugar, melt and caramelize the sugar in each ramekin. Serve immediately.

"I don't ever worry about the other team—they have to face me."

ON THE MENU
EMPANADAS
TOSTONES
TRIPLE CHOCOLATE BROWNIES

HANLEY RAMIREZ

SHORTSTOP FLORIDA MARLINS

★ No one would ever accuse Hanley Ramirez of lacking confidence. Undoubtedly, his presence on the field and at the plate is often intimidating to some of his opponents. Ramirez has what it takes to be one of the best players in baseball—not only a touch of bravado but also raw talent. Three consecutive years as an All-Star, winner of two Silver Slugger Awards, a National League Batting champion, and a National League Rookie of the Year, Ramirez is the celebrated shortstop for the Florida Marlins, and he's only just beginning.

Born and raised in the Dominican Republic, a launchpad for many notable Major League players, Ramirez played baseball tirelessly as a kid. He recalls, "I think it was like two days a week. From two o'clock until six or seven p.m. That was a league. Besides that, I played with friends at home every day." But for Ramirez, baseball became more than an after-school activity. Before long, word got around and Major League scouts quickly took notice of the young and exceptionally gifted athlete. At just sixteen years old, Ramirez signed with the Boston Red Sox and was well on his way to the Big Leagues.

At the beginning of his career, Ramirez had the added challenge of living apart from his family in a foreign country. "When I came to the United States, I missed my mom," he says. "But I used to call her every day. That was hard. I didn't have any family or friends here, just teammates." Veteran teammates and coaches gave Ramirez straightforward advice along the way. "You're here because you know what you want. You want to play in the Big Leagues," is the advice Ramirez remembers the most.

Still, for Ramirez, the journey to the Major Leagues seems like it was easy compared to the pressure of staying in the game, at the top. "A lot of preparation is needed and you have to be ready every day," he says.

"If I couldn't have rice, chicken, and beans I would have grown up in a different country. I love it, you know."

Today, Ramirez proudly remains close to his family and friends from home. In fact, Ramirez is all about family. "Being with my family is important to me," he says. "I like to have all of my family around me." Every baseball season, his parents visit south Florida from the Dominican Republic. "They come for a couple months and then go back to the Dominican and then come back again here," he explains.

Ramirez, who is a devoted father to his two young sons, Hanley Jr. and Hansel, and newborn daughter Hailey, is just as comfortable in his parenting role as he is playing short-stop. After a game is over, Ramirez can often be seen with Hanley Jr. and Hansel trailing close behind him in the clubhouse or playing an informal game of catch with them in the stadium parking lot—along with his teammates' kids, too. As for a future in baseball for Ramirez's two sons, he says, "If they want to; it's not like I'm going to push them into it." It is obvious to anyone who knows Ramirez that kids, his own or not, play an essential role in his life. In the near future, Ramirez is planning to expand his reach by launching a foundation for children in need.

Ramirez is in the midst of an exciting career, but he prefers a quiet life at home with family. And even though he has lived in the United States for more than ten years, he has not acquired an overwhelming fondness for traditional American food. "I don't like hot dogs or hamburgers much," he says. But he admits to liking plain cheese pizza and he has a weakness for warm brownies topped with vanilla ice cream and caramel.

Above all, Ramirez favors meals from his Dominican upbringing. At the top of his list are his beloved rice, chicken, and beans. He says, "If I couldn't have rice, chicken, and beans I would have grown up in a different country. I love it, you know." Before driving to the ballpark, Ramirez enjoys a leisurely midday meal of rice, chicken, and beans, with his wife and sons. Since he does not like to eat just before a game, he relies on his favorite lunch to give him the fuel to play long and hard, well into the evening hours.

Ramirez also loves twice-fried plantains, a dish more commonly known in Latin America as *tostones*. Ramirez even prides himself on being able to make them. "My mother taught me how to make them when I was younger," he says. When hungry for a snack, Ramirez will often fry up some tostones. Another food favorite from home is empanadas stuffed with vegetables, cheese, or chicken.

There's a lot going on for this All-Star shortstop, including the marketing of his personal style into his own H2R brand (HR for Hanley Ramirez and 2 for his uniform number). More recently, he's been expanding H2R into a retail business with a newly developed clothing line. And he is extremely serious about wanting to be an actor after baseball. "I want to be a movie star," he reveals. But for now, Hollywood will have to wait for Hanley Ramirez.

EMPANADAS

MAKES 15 EMPANADAS

★ When Hanley Ramirez travels to St. Louis to play against the Cardinals, he sometimes enjoys an authentic empanada made special from Deidre Pujols's kitchen. Many cooks don't bother with making the empanada dough from scratch, using frozen pastry rounds (*discos*), widely available in the frozen section at Latino grocers. There are two kinds—plain and orange-colored *achiote* (*annatto*)—and you can use either. If you can't find *discos,* use any pie dough, homemade or premade refrigerated, rolled out to $^1/_8$-inch thickness and cut into 5-inch rounds.

Filling

2 tablespoons olive oil

8 ounces ground round (85% lean)

½ teaspoon garlic salt

1 small yellow onion, finely chopped

½ medium green bell pepper, seeded and cut into ¼-inch dice

1 ripe medium tomato, seeded and chopped

3 garlic cloves, minced

1 beef bouillon cube, crushed

½ teaspoon ground cumin

½ teaspoon chili powder

1 teaspoon freshly squeezed orange juice

½ teaspoon distilled white vinegar

Salt and freshly ground black pepper

Empanadas

15 frozen empanada *discos* (1½ packages), thawed

Vegetable oil, for deep-frying

1 Heat 1 tablespoon of olive oil in a medium skillet over medium heat. Add the ground round and garlic salt. Cook, stirring often and breaking up the meat with the side of a wooden spoon, until the meat loses its raw look, about 8 minutes. Drain the beef mixture in a colander; set aside.

2 Add the remaining 1 tablespoon olive oil to the skillet and heat over medium heat. Add the onion, green pepper, tomato, garlic, bouillon cube, cumin, chili powder, orange juice, and vinegar. Cook, stirring often, until tender, about 8 minutes. Stir in the drained ground round and cook to blend the flavors, about 5 minutes. Season with salt and pepper, but you might not need much because of the salty bouillon. Transfer to a bowl and let cool completely.

3 Place a heaping tablespoon of the cooled filling on the bottom half of a *disco*. Brush the edges of the *disco* with water. Fold the *disco* in half to enclose the filling. Press the edges closed with the tines of a fork. Place on a baking sheet.

4 Pour vegetable oil into a large skillet to come halfway up the sides and heat over high heat to 350ºF. Line a baking sheet with a paper bag and place near the stove.

5 In batches, without crowding them, deep-fry the empanadas, turning halfway through cooking, until golden brown, about 2½ minutes. Using a wire spider or a slotted spoon, transfer the empanadas to the paper to drain. Serve warm or at room temperature.

[**BAKED EMPANADAS:** Instead of deep-frying them, bake the empanadas on baking sheets in a preheated 400ºF oven 15 to 20 minutes, until golden brown.

TOSTONES

MAKES 6–8 SERVINGS

★ Plantains are closely related to bananas, but they are larger, with very tough skin, and not as sweet—they are really more like a potato than a fruit. Because of their dense consistency, plantains are never eaten raw, but rather are steamed, fried, baked, or boiled. Tostones are plantains that are fried twice to give them a crunchiness that puts potato chips to shame. A special press is used to flatten the plantains into waffled chips, but the pointed end of a meat pounder or the bottom of a measuring cup works well, too (although your tostones won't be perforated). Here's what I learned from my personal tostones-making lesson from Hanley Ramirez.

4 green plantains (see Note)
Vegetable oil, for deep-frying
Salt

1 Trim off the tip and stem of each plantain. Cut into the skin of each plantain, using the tip of a sharp paring knife, following the ridges that run the length of the plantain and reaching just into the plantain flesh. Slip your thumb underneath the skin (you may need to make another incision between the skin and flesh to get started), and remove the skin in sections. Trim off any skin left on the flesh. Cut the plantains into 1-inch chunks.

2 Pour oil into a large, heavy skillet to come halfway up the sides and heat over high heat to 350°F. Line a large plate or small platter with paper towels.

3 In batches, without crowding, deep-fry the plantains, turning once, until light golden brown on both sides, about 5 minutes. Using a wire spider or slotted spoon, transfer the fried plantain chunks to the paper towels to drain and cool slightly, about 5 minutes.

4 Using the bottom of a measuring cup, apply pressure to individual plantain chunks to flatten each into a chip about ¼ inch thick.

5 Reheat the oil to 350°F. In batches, deep-fry the flattened plantains until very crisp and golden brown, about 3 minutes. Using the wire spider, return the tostones to the paper towels to drain. Season with salt and serve warm.

NOTE: Plantains are sold in three stages of ripeness: green (hard, unripe, and starchy), yellow (firm, ripe, and less starchy), and black (softening but not soft, very ripe, and very sweet).

TRIPLE CHOCOLATE BROWNIES

MAKES 12 LARGE BROWNIES

★ Ramirez is a serious brownie lover, so here's a recipe that is sure to get his approval. It is chocolate through and through, with chocolate chips inside and chocolate icing on top. Don't overbake the brownies, and they'll turn out nice and chewy. To serve them a la Hanley Ramirez, top your brownies with a scoop of ice cream and your favorite caramel sauce.

1 cup all-purpose flour, plus more for the pan

½ teaspoon baking soda

½ teaspoon salt

12 tablespoons (1½ sticks) unsalted butter, cut up, plus more for the pan

6 ounces unsweetened chocolate, finely chopped

1 cup packed light brown sugar

1 cup sugar

4 large eggs

2 teaspoons vanilla extract

3 cups (18 ounces) semisweet chocolate chips

1   Position a rack in the center of the oven and pre-heat to 350°F. Lightly butter the inside of a 13 x 9-inch baking pan. Line the bottom of the pan with a 24-inch length of aluminum foil, pleated down the center to fit the pan, letting the excess foil hang over the short ends of the pan. Butter the foil, then dust the inside of the pan with flour and tap out the excess.

2   Sift the flour, baking soda, and salt together. Melt the butter in a medium saucepan over medium heat. Remove from the heat and add the chocolate. Let stand for 3 minutes, then whisk to melt the chocolate. Whisk in the brown and granulated sugars. One at a time, beat in the eggs, then the vanilla. Add the flour mixture and stir until smooth. Stir in 1 cup of chocolate chips. Spread evenly in the pan.

3   Bake until a toothpick inserted near the center comes out with a moist crumb, about 35 minutes. Transfer the pan to a wire cake rack. Sprinkle the remaining 2 cups chocolate chips over the brownie and let stand 5 minutes to melt. Spread the melted chips in a thin layer on the brownie. Let cool completely in the pan.

4   Run a knife around the inside of the pan to loosen the brownie. Lift by the foil "handles" to remove the brownie from the pan in one piece. Cut into 12 brownies.

> "My first Major League game I saw in person was when I was seven or eight years old at Yankee Stadium. I sat in the third deck. I just remember how amazing it was to have green grass in the middle of the Bronx and being in this great building . . . It was beautiful."

ALEX RODRIGUEZ

THIRD BASEMAN NEW YORK YANKEES

★ Alex Rodriguez is one of the most accomplished players in the history of baseball. The New York–born, Dominican Republic–bred superstar debuted in Seattle as a promising young talent with unlimited range, skillful glovework, savvy base running, and power at the plate. During his first full season in the Majors, he emerged as an All-Star, winning the American League batting title with a .358 average.

Now, with well more than a decade's worth of Major League milestones, Rodriguez concedes that his ultimate baseball wish has remained the same year after year: "Winning the world championship and being part of that team." The current Yankees third baseman—having spent nearly half his life playing professional baseball—got his ultimate prize in 2009, when his team won a World Series Championship. "Nothing compares to winning a World Series," he says. "It was better than I ever imagined. It is the one thing in baseball where everyone is a winner, from the players to the manager, to the coaches and the fans. Everyone is happy."

The following year, Rodriguez achieved perhaps his most impressive individual milestone thus far: In 2010, on the sunny afternoon of August 4, the thirty-five-year-old megastar became the seventh player—and the youngest player in history—to hit 600 home runs. Yet even more remarkable is that Rodriguez's 600th home run occurred not only three years to the day after he hit his 500th home run, but it was also during a day game and his first at bat—the same circumstances under which he hit his 500th home run.

It is no wonder that Rodriguez's favorite baseball sound is the whack of the ball off a wooden bat during a home run swing. "It sounds amazing," he says. And if anyone knows that sound, it is surely Rodriguez.

135

"I'm a salt guy. That's my weakness. I love chips, but baked chips, and any type of nuts."

Like many baseball players, Rodriguez believes that consistent hitting starts with a familiar routine. "I take the same route to the plate and then I take two practice swings and then I go," he says. Off the field, Rodriguez surrounds himself with fine art and books. His love of art started with buying prints by modern masters like Chagall and Picasso, but he is now eager to explore a whole lot more of the art world, including contemporary artists like Basquiat and Warhol. He also collects photographs, including vintage prints of baseball greats like Lou Gehrig, Yogi Berra, Babe Ruth, and Joe DiMaggio. "I have a great picture of Gehrig and Ruth fishing in Canada," he says. "I love those pictures that are not uniform pictures."

Rodriguez also derives inspiration from reading, especially autobiographies and books on business. He says, "Every day when I wake up, I want to learn something new. I try to surround myself with the smartest people. I've always said that I want to be next to the smartest guy in the room and take in all his information like a sponge."

Closer to home, Rodriguez helps others learn and further their education. For the past fifteen years, he has been actively involved with the Boys and Girls Clubs of Miami-Dade County, raising money and opening the Alex Rodriguez Learning Center on one of its campuses. In addition, he provides full-tuition scholarships at the University of Miami.

Rodriguez has also made some marks with his keen business sense, including his primary involvement in real estate and auto dealership ventures. Owning a Major League Baseball club is top on his list of aspirations. And Rodriguez's interests and quest for knowledge do not end there. Every off-season he travels to Europe for a two-week immersion in culture, sightseeing, and good food. He cites Venice in the rain as one of his favorite destinations.

When it comes to eating, Rodriguez has very healthy habits, including his preference for organic food. He starts his day with a simple and healthy breakfast of fruit, brown rice, and scrambled egg whites. Whether he is on the road with the team or at home, he says that he always starts the day with that bowl of fruit. For a pregame meal, Rodriguez has his routine: five slices of turkey, no bread, and a sweet potato—just half—with "no oil, no butter, no nothing." Rodriguez eats sensibly, especially when it comes to dinner. "I like a three-course meal," he says. "I like to take my time eating." Soup is an especially nourishing start to a good meal for Rodriguez: "I love soup, any great food has to start with a good soup for me." And a salad of simple mixed greens topped with a simple balsamic dressing is standard for the All-Star third baseman.

For the most part, Rodriguez sticks to a healthy regimen of fish and vegetables such as steamed spinach or asparagus—plain without oil, butter, or salt. And like many great athletes, the uber-healthy and fit Rodriguez can't resist a really good steak every now

and then. He says, "I actually love a T-bone. I just crush and devour it." And perhaps not surprisingly, Rodriguez is not a dessert guy, easily able to skip sweets. He says, "I am a salt guy. That's my weakness. I love chips, but baked chips, and nuts, any type of nuts."

Just as he enjoys salty food, what Rodriguez hopes for in life is salt of the earth: "Just complete happiness, positive energy, and to try to make a conscious effort to make the world a better place." The Yankee great is just a regular guy who admits to not being perfect and is humbled by his mistakes. At the end of the day, baseball All-Stars are people, too.

GRILLED T-BONE STEAKS WITH BALSAMIC ONION CONFIT

MAKES 4 SERVINGS

★ There aren't many dishes more satisfying than a sizzling steak with a full complement of savory side dishes. Alex Rodriguez likes his sides tasty and free of unnecessary fat and calories. This slow-cooked confit (a French culinary term referring to an ingredient slowly cooked in its own juices) fits the bill, and leftovers can be refrigerated for the next day. Add some steamed spinach and oven-roasted sweet potatoes as a well-balanced complement to the steaks, and you've got a dinner that knocks it out of the park.

Balsamic Onion Confit

1 tablespoon unsalted butter

3 large onions, peeled and sliced about ½ inch thick

Pinch of salt

3 tablespoons balsamic vinegar

3 tablespoons honey, preferably acacia honey

Steaks

4 14-ounce T-bone steaks

½ teaspoons salt

½ teaspoon freshly ground black pepper

1 To make the onions, melt the butter in a nonstick large skillet over medium heat. Add the onions and salt and stir well. Add 1 cup water. Cook, stirring often, until the water evaporates and the onions are softened, about 20 minutes. Stir another cup of water into the onions. Cook, stirring often, until the water evaporates and the onions are tender and beginning to brown, about 20 minutes more.

2 Stir in the vinegar and honey. Cook, stirring often to avoid scorching, until the onions are caramelized and the liquids are syrupy, about 10 minutes. Remove from the heat and cover the skillet to keep the onions warm.

3 Meanwhile, prepare a hot fire in an outdoor grill. Season the steaks with the salt and pepper and let stand at room temperature while the grill heats.

4 Lightly oil the grill grate. Place the steaks on the grill and cover. Grill, turning after 3½ minutes, until the tops of the steaks feel somewhat firmer than raw when pressed with a finger, about 7 minutes for medium-rare steak.

5 Transfer each steak to a dinner plate. Top with a heap of onions and serve at once.

BAKED KALE CHIPS

MAKES 4–6 SERVINGS

★ Alex Rodriguez eats sensibly, and that includes plenty of nutritious leafy greens. But he also can't resist a bowl of crunchy baked chips when it comes to a snack. As a healthier alternative to potato chips, try these homemade kale chips that will have your guests asking "Is this *really* kale?" Use lacinato kale, which has very curly, dark green leaves. Look for it at your natural foods market or well-stocked supermarkets.

1 10-ounce bunch lacinato kale
2 tablespoons extra-virgin olive oil
Salt

1 Position a rack in the center of the oven and pre-heat to 375°F.

2 Pull off the rib from each kale leaf. Wash the kale and spin in a salad spinner. Some water droplets will remain in the curls of the leaves; pat dry with paper towels and let kale air dry for an hour or so. The kale leaves should be as dry as possible.

3 Spread the leaves on two rimmed baking sheets. Drizzle each sheet with 1 tablespoon oil, and toss leaves to coat with the oil. Arrange the leaves so they overlap as little as possible.

4 Bake, 1 sheet at a time, just until the kale becomes crisp, 8–10 minutes. Do not overcook the kale or it could become bitter. Sprinkle the kale with salt. Transfer the chips to a platter or a deep bowl (they are less likely to break on a platter) and serve.

CHICKEN VEGETABLE SOUP WITH BROWN RICE

MAKES 8 SERVINGS

★ There is a tradition of making long-simmered chicken soup with a tough old bird, but younger poultry works just as well and cooks up in much less time. The trick is to remove the tender parts when they are done, leaving the bony pieces in the pot to release more flavor. Here's a chicken soup for Alex Rodriguez. He loves a good soup, especially a clear broth filled with chunks of tender vegetables and chicken, bolstered with nutritious brown rice.

2 tablespoons vegetable oil

1 3½-pound chicken, giblets reserved (discard the liver), cut into 2 wings, 2 breast halves, 2 drumsticks, 2 thighs, and 1 back

2 medium leeks, white and pale green parts only, well-washed and chopped (2 cups)

2 medium carrots, cut into ¼-inch rounds

2 medium celery ribs with leaves, cut into ¼-inch slices, leaves chopped

½ teaspoon dried thyme

4 sprigs of fresh parsley

1 bay leaf

Salt and freshly ground black pepper

½ cup brown rice

Chopped fresh parsley, for garnish

1 Heat the oil in a large pot over medium-high heat. In batches, add the chicken and cook, turning occasionally, until lightly browned, about 6 minutes. Transfer to a plate. Don't bother to brown the giblets.

2 Discard all but 1 tablespoon of the oil from the pot and return to medium heat. Add the leeks, carrots, and celery and cover. Cook, stirring occasionally, until the vegetables soften, about 5 minutes. Return the chicken to the pot and add enough water to cover the chicken by 1 inch, about 2½ quarts. Bring to a boil over high heat, skimming off any fat that rises to the surface. Add the thyme, parsley sprigs, and bay leaf. Season with 1 teaspoon salt and ½ teaspoon pepper.

3 Reduce the heat to medium-low. Simmer, uncovered, until the breast halves are cooked through, about 45 minutes. Transfer the breast halves to a plate and set aside until easy to handle. Continue simmering the broth with the drumsticks, thighs, wings, backs, and giblets until the broth is full-flavored, 30–45 minutes more. Using tongs, remove the drumsticks and thighs and set aside to cool. Remove and discard the wings, back, and giblets.

4 When the chicken is cool, remove the skin and bones, cut the meat into bite-size pieces, and stir the meat back into the pot.

5 Meanwhile, bring 1½ cups water, the brown rice, and ½ teaspoon salt to a boil in a medium saucepan over high heat. Reduce the heat to low and tightly cover the saucepan. Cook until the rice is tender and has absorbed the water, about 45 minutes. Remove from the heat and let stand, covered, for 5 minutes.

6 Stir the brown rice into the soup. Remove the parsley sprigs and bay leaf. Season with salt and pepper. Ladle into bowls, sprinkle with chopped parsley, and serve hot.

JOHAN SANTANA

PITCHER NEW YORK METS

★ With an array of unhittable pitching combinations in his arsenal, Johan Santana, the New York Mets ace, is one of the fiercest pitchers in baseball. Since becoming a Major League success, Santana has racked up two Cy Young Awards and is a recurrent All-Star. And he continues to bring his enthusiasm to the game. "I cannot wait to go out there every time that I'm pitching. I am always excited about baseball, always willing to play, and I wish I could play every day, and I wish I could be on the field every single time," he says.

In Tovar, a remote Venezuelan town near the Andes Mountains where Santana grew up, it was all about soccer. "Baseball wasn't that big in my hometown," says Santana. But Santana wanted nothing more than to be a baseball player like his father. He says, "I always wanted to be like my dad, who played shortstop in a local baseball league. He used to take my brother and me to his games, and that's how I started playing. I learned from watching my dad."

Santana was a quick study, despite learning to play without the proper equipment: "When I started playing baseball, I was playing as a right-hander because the only equipment I had was my dad's. It was big, but that's the only thing I had. Once I started playing baseball on a Little League team, I found out I was left-handed and everything was much easier and I started playing baseball better."

When he was fifteen, Santana's baseball skills caught the eye of a Major League scout. "One time we had a national tournament and that's pretty much how everything started, in the national tournament with scouts watching. I didn't have a clue what a scout was, to

143

"Every time I go back home, I am dying for the food I grew up eating."

be honest with you," he says. But the scouts certainly knew about Santana. The next year, the Houston Astros welcomed the young phenom into their prestigious baseball academy.

Santana recalls, "I think that was the toughest thing I had done in my life, you know, leaving my family at fifteen years old to play baseball in another country. I didn't know English. I did not even know how to live without my parents. And when I saw my dad leaving, I was sad, but at the same time I took that as a challenge and my mindset was to make my family proud. I told myself that 'I'm going to try and do my best' and that was my mentality."

Though a long way from the mountains of Venezuela, Santana remains an active member of his hometown community through his charity, the Johan Santana Foundation. Whether his organization is sending much-needed supplies back home to the local hospital, the fire station, and other nearby communities, or donating thousands of gifts to young children during the holidays, Santana continues to give back.

And he never forgets the tastes of home, including his favorite childhood cuisine. In the off-season, he visits family and friends back in Tovar. "Every time I go back home, I am dying for the food I grew up eating," he says. And he adds proudly, "I haven't lost any of my traditions, no way. It is part of what I am and part of what we want our family to eat." As a kid, Santana helped out in his grandfather's bakery, including being the bread salesman. "I went to school from noon to 6 p.m. As a part-time job, in the mornings before school and on the weekends, I used to go to the bakery and work with my grandfather and uncles. I went to the flea market to sell bread that my grandfather and my uncles made. I used to follow people around trying to sell the bread. I would say that I was a good salesman. I would really put myself into it," he says.

Today he still often enjoys a home-cooked meal of *sancocho,* a Venezuelan meat stew. Santana remembers fondly the many occasions he helped his mother in the kitchen as a young boy, including husking corn or peeling yuccas for the weekly cooking of *sancocho.* He recalls with a smile, "Where I am from, we used to get together pretty much every week and make a *sancocho,* which is a soup made with ribs or chicken and vegetables, but we were not just making a little meal, we were making enough for all of our family together. We would all go to my parents' house or my grandparents' house and we got together as a family and cooked. That was pretty good."

Another popular dish today in the Santana household is a Venezuelan favorite called *reina pepiada,* an arepa stuffed with a mixture of chicken and avocado salad. And Santana's favorite dessert remains in the rotation—a topping of dulce de leche on a thin round wafer.

After pitching, however, Santana prefers lighter fare. A simple serving of warm soup is his go-to comfort food. "One thing that I really like a lot is soup, but home-cooked chicken

soup," he says. "I feel like after the game, I have to have something warm to make me relax and bring me back to life."

Beyond baseball, Santana's family brings him back to life, too. He says, "I just spend time with my family. It is the best thing to do to recover from a baseball season. We go out and play minigolf. I go to the supermarket . . . I still love to do all those things." And the All-Star is a softy when it comes to his young daughters. "There are times when we are in the house and my girls start brushing my hair and doing my nails, and I do that just to make them happy and make them laugh," he says.

As for life outside of baseball, Santana humbly says, "I am just another human being in this world who is trying to do his best to accomplish a lot of things in life . . . not just baseball." And for baseball fans everywhere, this is surely food for thought.

REINA PEPIADA AREPAS

MAKES 6 AREPAS

⭐ Arepas define Venezuelan cooking. These thick cornmeal patties are griddled, then baked, and then stuffed while warm with anything from white cheese to this zesty chicken salad with avocado mayonnaise (Johan Santana's first choice). The salad is named in honor of Susana Duijm, Miss World in 1955 and a popular Venezuelan celebrity. (*Reina* means "queen" in Spanish, and *pepiada* is perhaps most politely translated as "curvy.") The recipe comes from Maribel Araujo of New York's always-packed Caracas Arepa Bar in the East Village and her executive chef, Ilse Parra.

Filling

2 6-ounce skinless, boneless chicken breasts

½ small onion, sliced

Salt and freshly ground black pepper

1 ripe Hass avocado, pitted, peeled, and coarsely chopped

¼ cup mayonnaise

1 tablespoon distilled white vinegar, plus more to taste

2 tablespoons minced fresh cilantro

2 tablespoons minced fresh parsley

½ jalapeño, seeded and minced

2 garlic cloves, minced

½ cup seeded and diced (¼-inch) red bell pepper

2 tablespoons finely chopped red onion

1 scallion, white and green parts, finely chopped

Arepas

3 cups lukewarm water, or as needed

1¼ teaspoons salt

3 cups Venezuelan cornmeal, or as needed (see p. 147)

2 tablespoons plus 1 teaspoon canola or vegetable oil, plus more for the griddle

1 To make the filling, place the chicken breasts and onion in a medium saucepan and add enough cold water to cover by 1 inch. Add ½ teaspoon salt and ¼ teaspoon pepper and bring to a simmer over medium heat. Reduce the heat to medium-low and simmer, uncovered, until the chicken is cooked through, about 15 minutes. Remove the chicken from the saucepan and let cool completely. Tear the chicken into shreds.

2 Mash the avocado, mayonnaise, and vinegar together in a medium bowl with an immersion blender or large fork until smooth. Stir in the cilantro, parsley, jalapeño, and garlic. Add the chicken, red pepper, red onion, and scallion and mix together. Season with salt and pepper. Taste and add more vinegar to give the filling a pleasant, but not sour, tang. Cover and refrigerate until ready to serve.

3 To make the arepas, stir 3 cups lukewarm water and the salt together in a large bowl to dissolve the salt. Gradually add 3 cups cornmeal, mixing with your fingers to dissolve any lumps, adding enough to make a soft dough that holds its shape without cracking when molded. Set dough aside to rest for 3 minutes. Add the oil and work it in with your hands, adding cornmeal or water to return the dough to the proper consistency.

4 Divide the dough into 6 equal portions. Shape each into a 4-inch diameter disk, about 1 inch thick. Transfer to a baking sheet.

5 Position a rack in the center of the oven and preheat the oven to 350°F. Lightly oil a large nonstick skillet or griddle and heat over medium heat.

6 In batches, place the arepas in the skillet. Cook until the underside is a splotchy golden brown, about 4 minutes. Turn and brown the other side. Return arepas to the baking sheet.

7 When all of the arepas are browned, transfer them directly to the oven rack (without the baking sheet). Bake until the surfaces of the arepas have formed a taut skin—if you rap your fingers on one, it will feel and sound like a drum. Return arepas to the baking sheet and let cool slightly. Split each arepa in half and fill with the chicken mixture. Serve warm.

NOTE: For arepas, you must use precooked cornmeal (labeled *harina* or *harina precocida*), imported from Venezuela. American cornmeal or corn flour and Mexican *masa harina* will not work. The most popular brand of precooked cornmeal is P.A.N., found at Latino markets or online at www.amigofoods.com. Use white (*blanco*)

SANCOCHO

MAKES 10–12 SERVINGS

⭐ *Sancocho* is a rib-sticking stew made from beef or chicken with lots of vegetables to fill you up. It was one of Johan Santana's favorite dishes growing up in Venezuela, and it remains one of his family's top meal choices today. This recipe makes plenty, so unless you have a big crowd to feed, plan on freezing some for another meal or two.

2½ pounds stewing beef with bones, such as cross-cut short ribs or beef shanks

1 medium red bell pepper, seeded and chopped

1 beef bouillon cube, crushed

½ teaspoon dried oregano

½ teaspoon garlic salt

8 scallions, trimmed and thinly sliced

¼ cup chopped fresh cilantro

1 tablespoon chopped fresh parsley or ½ teaspoon dried parsley, plus more fresh parsley for serving

Salt and freshly ground black pepper

2 pounds yucca, peeled and cut into 1-inch chunks

2 yellow plantains, peeled and chopped into 1-inch rounds (see page 132)

1 pound butternut squash, peeled, seeded, and cut into 1-inch pieces

4 ears of corn, each cut crosswise into 4 rounds

Cooked white rice (see page 123), for serving

1 Combine the beef, red pepper, bouillon cube, oregano, and garlic salt in a large soup pot. Add enough water to cover the ingredients by 2 inches, about 3 quarts. Bring to a boil over high heat, skimming off any foam that rises to the surface. Add the scallions, cilantro, parsley, 1 teaspoon salt, and ½ teaspoon pepper. Reduce the heat to medium-low and simmer uncovered for 1 hour.

2 Stir in the yucca, plantains, butternut squash, and corn. Simmer until the beef and root vegetables are tender, about 1 hour longer. Season with salt and pepper.

3 Ladle stew into bowls, garnish with fresh parsley, and serve with a side dish of rice.

DULCE DE LECHE OVER VANILLA ICE CREAM WITH BUTTERED PECANS

MAKES 4 SERVINGS

★ Dulce de leche, Latin America's fabulously delicious contribution to the world of desserts, is essentially condensed milk that is slowly cooked until it turns a deep caramelized beige color. Johan Santana enjoys dulce de leche simply spread on the Venezuelan wafer cookies called *obleas*, but this recipe transforms simple vanilla ice cream into so much more. You'll find dulce de leche at specialty food shops, at Latino grocers, and by mail order from www.bodeguita.com.

1 tablespoon unsalted butter

1 cup pecan halves

2 teaspoons sugar

¼ teaspoon salt

1 13.4-ounce can dulce de leche

1 pint vanilla ice cream

6 thin wafer cookies, such as *obleas*, or rolled Pirouette cookies, optional

1 Melt the butter in a medium nonstick skillet over medium heat. Add the pecans, sugar, and salt. Cook, stirring often, until the pecans smell toasted and the sugar has melted, about 2 minutes. Transfer to a plate and let cool. Coarsely chop the pecans.

2 Heat the dulce de leche in a small saucepan over low heat, stirring often, until warm and pourable. (Or heat in a microwave oven.)

3 Place 1 large scoop vanilla ice cream into each bowl. Drizzle with about ¼ cup of the warm dulce de leche and a generous sprinkle of the pecans. Serve at once.

"I'm just proud to be playing the game I love. I think I am one of the fortunate ones who get to make a career out of a hobby that I played as a kid. So just to be playing here and making a career out of this and doing what I love is just something I will always remember."

GRADY SIZEMORE

OUTFIELDER CLEVELAND INDIANS

★ Before he became a Major League Baseball player, Grady Sizemore was also a standout high school basketball and football player. Having been a three-sport star athlete in his formative years, Sizemore is a natural competitor. The unassuming Cleveland Indians outfielder is refreshingly nonchalant about whether excelling at multiple sports has made him a superstar baseball player. "I think it definitely helps you be a better athlete, but I don't know if it translates into how I am playing today," he says. "I'm sure it couldn't hurt. I think for me, it was just what I wanted to do. I didn't really think about how it would affect me in the future. It was just one of those things I enjoyed doing."

Sizemore's career began just out of high school as a Montreal Expos early draft pick. Two years later he was traded to the Cleveland Indians, where he made his Major League debut. The next year, the promising young outfielder's game kept improving. He became a three-time All-Star, a two-time Gold Glove, and a Silver Slugger, all in less than four years. Sizemore admits that baseball is the main priority in his life right now. He says, "I can't say I have much going on besides baseball. It's pretty much year-round for me, and other than my family and friends, it's all I focus on." And although sidelined with injuries through part of his 2009 and 2010 seasons, Sizemore remains undeterred about regaining his All-Star status. He says, "I don't have too many worries. I think there is nothing much I really worry about." Does he miss being part of the action? You bet. "Not since middle school have I had this much time where I was not playing baseball," he says.

"It's two eggs over medium, bacon, wheat toast with just butter and waffles plain or with fruit, pretty much every day."

During the baseball season, many players develop their own unique routines. Sizemore has a habit of wearing the same clothes every day. "I have certain socks that I wear, certain sliders I wear, undershirts I wear, that's all the same every day until there are holes in them," he explains. His other routine is breakfast. "It's two eggs over medium, bacon, wheat toast with just butter and waffles plain or with fruit, pretty much every day," he says. "In the off-season it is not quite as big."

Though Sizemore's off-season home is now Scottsdale, Arizona, he was born and raised in Seattle. "I like Seattle; I grew up there and I still like going there. They have great food and you can always get fresh fish there," he says. And true to his Seattle roots, Sizemore is a really cool, laid-back guy with great taste in alternative music—and a penchant for good coffee, though he admits to only recently joining the ranks of serious coffee drinkers. He says, "It's funny, I didn't drink it until I started playing baseball. I just like to drink it in the morning. I go cream and sugar, heavy cream, heavy sugar." In the winter months, he likes watching the Discovery Channel with a cup of coffee in hand and his dog, Carmella, by his side. "She's a sweetheart," he says of his five-year-old pit bull.

While living in Scottsdale, Sizemore is near family and friends. His younger brother lives nearby, and his parents are twenty minutes away. "We all have dinner together about three times a week," he says. And as a bachelor, Sizemore is quite at home in the kitchen. Although he bats and throws left-handed, he eats, chops food, grills, and writes with his right hand. "And I am right-footed," he adds. Regarding his cooking repertoire, he says, "I've got three or four meals I make. I like to grill steak, a T-bone, a Porterhouse, or whatever I can get. I grill halibut, cook spaghetti, and I do a chicken and pasta dish that I can make with an Alfredo sauce or a tomato-based sauce. My mom likes it, and I make it for her," he says with a laugh. But Sizemore fancies his mother's cooking the most. Among Mom's winning meals is a layered bean dip that is so simple to make that even Sizemore mastered the recipe. "I called my mother from the grocery store for the ingredients and made it for a friend's party. No one believed that I made it," he says. Other favorite family recipes include chili, cornbread, and chocolate cake. "There is no shortage of carbs in my family," adds Sizemore.

Another little-known fact is that Sizemore is not a fan of messiness. "I'm kind of a neat freak. Everything has to be in its place—on the outside. The closets, however, are just chaos and the drawers are chaos, but appearance-wise it looks neat . . . but if you dig deep you might find a little bit of a mess," he says with a laugh.

When it comes to All-Star outfielder Grady Sizemore, you don't have to dig too deep to grasp that he is an outstanding athlete and a great guy.

AUNT TONYA'S CHILI

MAKES 6–8 SERVINGS

★ Chili is another dish that ballplayers universally love. This is the way Sizemore's Aunt Tonya makes her nourishing ground beef version. If you like a thicker chili, stir a few tablespoons of yellow cornmeal into the pot at the end of the cooking time.

2 pounds ground round (85% lean)

2 tablespoons vegetable oil

1 large onion, chopped

4 garlic cloves, minced

1 jalapeño, seeded and minced

3 tablespoons chili powder

1 teaspoon ground cumin

1 15-ounce can tomato sauce

1 15-ounce can vegetarian refried beans

1 6-ounce can tomato paste

½ cup green salsa

1 19-ounce can kidney beans, drained and rinsed

12 ounces lager beer

Salt and freshly ground pepper, to taste

Hot red pepper sauce, to taste

Shredded mild cheddar, sour cream, and tortilla chips, for serving

1 Cook the ground round in a Dutch oven or flame-proof casserole over medium-high heat, stirring often and breaking up the meat with the side of a spoon, until it loses its raw look, about 10 minutes. Drain in a colander.

2 Heat the oil in the Dutch oven over medium heat. Add the onion, garlic, and jalapeño and cook, stirring occasionally, until the onion is tender, about 5 minutes. Return the ground round to the Dutch oven, sprinkle with the chili powder and cumin, and stir well. Stir in 1½ cups water, the tomato sauce, refried beans, tomato paste, and salsa and bring to a simmer. Reduce the heat to medium-low and cover. Simmer for 20 minutes.

3 Stir in the kidney beans and beer. Simmer until the sauce is slightly thickened, 15–20 minutes. Season with salt and pepper and hot red pepper sauce.

4 Ladle the chili into bowls and serve with the cheddar, sour cream, and tortilla chips on the side.

WARM REFRIED BEAN DIP

MAKES 6–8 SERVINGS

★ This basic and easy family recipe is from Sizemore's mother, Donna: "It is yummy and Grady loves it—although he does pick off the olives." It is a real crowd-pleaser, according to the Sizemore family. With sour cream, cheese, and salsa, how can you go wrong?

2 16-ounce cans vegetarian refried beans
1 16-ounce container sour cream
1 16-ounce jar medium-hot salsa (not thick and chunky)
2 cups (8 ounces) shredded sharp cheddar
1 2.25-ounce can sliced black olives
Tortilla chips, for servings

1 Position a rack in the center of the oven and pre-heat to 350°F.

2 Spread the refried beans in an 11½ x 8-inch bak-ing dish. Mix the sour cream and salsa together, and spread over the beans. Sprinkle with the cheddar cheese, then the olives.

3 Bake until the dip is bubbling and the cheese is melted, about 25 minutes. Let cool at room tempera-ture for 20 minutes. Serve warm, with the tortilla chips for dipping.

[
COLD REFRIED BEAN DIP: This dip is also great served cold. If you wish, add a layer of diced avocado on top of the cheese.

CORNBREAD

MAKES 6–8 SERVINGS

★ Cornbread is welcome at any time of the day, filling the kitchen with sweet baked aromas. This easy recipe, which literally takes just a few minutes to stir up, comes from Sizemore's mother, Donna. Serve it at breakfast drizzled with honey and butter, at lunch with soup or salad, or for dinner with a big pot of chili.

¾ cup all-purpose flour
3 tablespoons sugar
1¼ teaspoons baking powder
1 teaspoon salt
½ teaspoon baking soda
1½ cups yellow cornmeal
1½ cups buttermilk
2 large eggs, beaten
¼ cup vegetable oil, plus more for the skillet

1 Position a rack in the center of the oven and pre-heat the oven to 400°F. Lightly oil a 9- or 10-inch ovenproof skillet.

2 Sift the flour, sugar, baking powder, salt, and baking soda together into a large bowl. Stir in the cornmeal. Whisk the buttermilk, eggs, and oil together in another bowl. Add to the flour mixture and stir just until com-bined. Do not overmix. Spread in the skillet.

3 Bake until golden brown and the top springs back when pressed in the center, about 30 minutes. Let stand at room temperature for 5 minutes, then cut into wedges and serve warm, right from the skillet.

> "I feel like I've worked extremely hard going all the way back to high school. Practicing a lot. Extremely motivated, actually. And I love the game, so I think that makes it easier."

CHASE UTLEY

SECOND BASEMAN PHILADELPHIA PHILLIES

★ The beginning of the 2011 baseball season marked nine years since Chase Utley made his Major League debut for the Philadelphia Phillies. The five-time All-Star second baseman and four-time Silver Slugger is enormously driven and disciplined. He is one of the first players to arrive at the ballpark to prepare for a game. "I arrive early all the time," he says. "It was a habit I got into probably right when I got to the Big Leagues. Showing up early, I have a routine that I kind of go through on a daily basis. I don't like to rush through things, so I'd rather have a little downtime on the field than rush."

Utley's no-rush attitude was evident during his transition from amateur to professional baseball. As a Southern California native, he grew up rooting for the Los Angeles Dodgers and was drafted by his favorite team in his senior year of high school. But characteristic of his methodical makeup, Utley opted for college instead. Utley recalls, "I remember it was a great opportunity to play for my hometown team that I grew up watching. I was drafted fairly high, so it was a good situation to be in, but I realized that if baseball was meant to be, then it would be there after college. I wanted to go to college, attempt to get an education, make some friends, and have a good time, and that's what I did." The son of an attorney, Utley enrolled at UCLA as a history major, but he emphatically states that he did not have any desire to follow in his father's footsteps and become a lawyer. Luckily for his fans, Utley's clear thinking about his route to the pros through college proved correct. After attending UCLA, he was drafted by the Philadelphia Phillies. The next decade witnessed Utley becoming arguably the game's best second baseman and a natural team leader.

"I don't eat dessert as much anymore, but my favorite of all time is mud pie—it is unbelievable."

Utley attributes his strong work ethic and success in the game he loves to the coaches who helped him through the years, including back in his Little League days. "I've always had great coaches: growing up in Little League, in high school, in the Minor League system, and up here in the Big Leagues. I've always had coaches that I got along with, that had a lot to offer, and I just definitely think were great." Ask Utley about the best advice he ever received and he instantly quotes the late great Philadelphia coach John Vukovich: "Never take an inning off."

While Utley certainly has his hands full as an All-Star ballplayer, he rarely takes an inning off outside the ballpark. When he is not on the field, much of Utley's time is dedicated to raising awareness for the Pennsylvania Society for the Prevention of Cruelty to Animals (PSPCA). He grew up surrounded by animals, so his interest in the PSPCA was a natural fit. "My family had a bunch of animals when I was growing up. We had birds, dogs, cats, rabbits, turtles, and iguanas. My mom was a huge animal person," says Utley. Over three years, Utley has raised an impressive amount of financial support for the PSPCA to help end animal abuse. He has even rescued several abused and neglected animals himself, including adopting a dog, Jack, and two cats, Sugar and Sebastian.

With his beloved dog, Jack, constantly by his side, Utley gets ready for his day with almond butter and jelly on a toasted pita. He also makes his own coffee, but healthy eating is what fuels Utley's full and organized days: "Usually, I have an almond butter and jelly sandwich on wheat bread. Every day, for the most part." And he adds, "I like all fruit, except I'm not a big cantaloupe or honeydew guy." And his favorite sandwich is roasted turkey with avocado and mustard—no mayonnaise ever—with a side dish of quinoa. To quench his thirst before or after a game, Utley prefers coconut water: "I have a lot of it. So far, I am into it because it is supposed to hydrate you more than regular water." Utley claims to be "a big sushi fan," and he is also a fan of homemade risotto and roast chicken. As for the occasional dessert, Utley says, "I don't eat dessert as much anymore, but my favorite of all time is mud pie—it is unbelievable."

And, to Philadelphia baseball fans, so is Chase Utley.

ROAST CHICKEN WITH AUTUMN VEGETABLES

MAKES 4 SERVINGS

★ You can serve roast chicken any time of year, and it is one of Chase Utley's favorite meals. This is how I make roast chicken, with the vegetables and chicken baked together to exchange flavors. The chicken is finished with a light glaze of balsamic vinegar, adding a little sweetness to the natural sugars in the vegetables. Always let roast chicken stand for at least 10 minutes before carving so the juices have a chance to settle.

1 4-pound chicken, giblets removed, rinsed and patted dry

2 tablespoons unsalted butter, at room temperature

Salt and freshly ground black pepper

2 medium yellow onions, 1 whole and 1 cut into quarters lengthwise

3 medium carrots, cut into 1-inch chunks

1 large parsnip, peeled and cut into 1-inch chunks

2 large baking potatoes, peeled and cut into 1-inch chunks

10 sprigs fresh thyme

5 sprigs fresh rosemary

2 tablespoons extra-virgin olive oil

8 whole garlic cloves, unpeeled

2 tablespoons aged balsamic vinegar (see Note)

1 Position a rack in the center of the oven and preheat to 400ºF. Lightly oil a large roasting pan.

2 Rub the chicken with the butter. Season inside and out with 1 teaspoon salt and ½ teaspoon pepper. Place the peeled whole onion in the body cavity. Season the outside of the chicken with salt and pepper, the thyme, and the rosemary. With butcher's twine, tie the legs together and tuck the chicken wings behind the body.

3 Place the quartered onion, carrots, parsnip, and potatoes in the roasting pan. Add the olive oil and 1 teaspoon salt and ½ teaspoon pepper and mix well, keeping the onion quarters intact. Place the chicken on top of the vegetables. Bake for 45 minutes. Stir the garlic into the vegetables. Continue roasting until an instant-read thermometer inserted in the thickest part of the thigh, not touching a bone, reads 165ºF, about 20 minutes longer. Remove the pan with the chicken and vegetables from the oven. Brush the chicken with the balsamic vinegar, and continue roasting until the internal temperature is 170ºF, about 10 minutes longer.

4 Transfer the chicken to a platter and let it stand 10 minutes before carving. Keep the vegetables warm in the turned-off oven. (If the vegetables aren't quite tender, continue roasting them while the chicken is standing.)

5 Season the vegetables with salt and pepper. Transfer to the platter and serve hot.

NOTE: For this recipe, use an aged balsamic vinegar, which is thicker and has more sweet, complex flavor than the usual supermarket balsamic. Alternatively, substitute 1 tablespoon honey mixed with 1 tablespoon balsamic vinegar for the aged vinegar.

QUINOA PILAF WITH ASPARAGUS AND GOLDEN RAISINS

MAKES 4 SERVINGS

★ Slightly chewy, with a delicious nutlike flavor, quinoa is a great grain to get to know, and it is part of Chase Utley's healthy eating routine. There are two colors, red and white, but they taste the same, and mixing them brings color to the table. In this pilaf, which can be served warm or at room temperature, I've added an interesting combination of asparagus and raisins, but I also make quinoa with blanched carrots and minced red onions.

12 asparagus spears, woody stems trimmed

½ cup white quinoa

½ cup red quinoa

½ cup coarsely chopped golden raisins, rinsed under hot water to soften slightly, drained

1 tablespoon freshly squeezed lemon juice

1 tablespoon extra-virgin olive oil

Salt and freshly ground black pepper

1 Bring a large saucepan of lightly salted water to a boil over high heat. Add the asparagus and cook until crisp-tender, about 4 minutes. Drain, reserving 1 cup of the asparagus cooking liquid. Rinse the asparagus under cold running water, drain again, and chop into 1-inch pieces. Set aside.

2 Bring the reserved asparagus water and a large pinch of salt to a boil in a medium saucepan over high heat. Combine the white and red quinoas in a fine-mesh wire sieve and rinse under cold water. (This removes the natural coating on the grains, which can be bitter.) Add to the boiling water and stir. Reduce the heat to medium-low and cover tightly.

3 Simmer until the water is almost completely absorbed, about 15 minutes. Add the asparagus and raisins to the saucepan, but do not stir. Cover, and continue cooking until the quinoa is tender, about 5 minutes more. Drain in the sieve.

4 Transfer quinoa mixture to a bowl. Sprinkle with the lemon juice and oil, season with salt and pepper, and mix. Serve warm or cooled to room temperature.

ULTIMATE MUD PIE

MAKES 8 SERVINGS

★ Chase Utley is not a dessert guy, unless it is mud pie. Once you try this incredible dessert recipe, you, too, will find your dinner guests unable to turn away a serving of bliss.

Chocolate Crumb Crust

1½ cups chocolate wafer cookie crumbs

3 tablespoons unsalted butter, melted, plus more for the pie pan

1 tablespoon sugar

Filling

3 cups half-and-half

⅔ cup sugar

⅛ teaspoon salt

¼ cup cornstarch

4 large egg yolks

5 ounces high-quality bittersweet or semisweet chocolate, finely chopped

2 tablespoons unsalted butter

½ teaspoon vanilla extract

Topping

1 cup heavy cream

2 tablespoons confectioners' sugar

½ teaspoon vanilla extract

2 tablespoons chocolate wafer crumbs, for garnish

1 Position a rack in the center of the oven and preheat the oven to 350°F. Lightly butter a 9-inch pie pan.

2 To make the crust, combine the crumbs, melted butter, and sugar in a medium bowl until moistened. Press firmly and evenly into the pie pan. Bake until the crust is set and smells like warm cookies, about 12 minutes. Cool completely.

3 To make the filling, in a medium saucepan over medium heat, heat 2½ cups of the half-and-half, the sugar, and the salt, stirring often to dissolve the sugar, until simmering. Pour into a heatproof bowl. Rinse out the saucepan.

4 In a small bowl, sprinkle the cornstarch over the remaining ½ cup half-and-half and whisk until dissolved. Whisk the yolks in a medium bowl, and gradually whisk in the cornstarch mixture. Gradually whisk in the hot half-and-half mixture and return to the rinsed-out saucepan. Cook over medium heat, stirring constantly with a flat wooden spatula (to keep the mixture from scorching), until it comes to a boil. Reduce the heat to medium-low and let the mixture bubble, stirring constantly, for 1 minute. Remove from the heat, add the chocolate, butter, and vanilla, and whisk until the chocolate melts completely. Strain through a wire sieve into a clean bowl.

5 Pour the filling into the cooled crust and press plastic wrap directly on the filling to keep a skin from forming. Let cool completely. Refrigerate until the filling is chilled and set, at least 2 hours.

6 To make the topping, whip the cream, confectioners' sugar, and vanilla in a chilled medium bowl with an electric mixer set on high speed until stiff. Uncover the pie. Spread and swirl the topping over the filling. (If you wish, transfer the whipped cream to a pastry bag fitted with a star tip, and pipe the cream onto the pie.) Sprinkle pie with cookie crumbs. Slice and serve chilled.

> "The one thing I love most about this game is that I get to be competitive for a living."

DAVID WRIGHT

THIRD BASEMAN NEW YORK METS

★ David Wright is undeniably one of the top players in the game. But it hasn't gone to his head. He is a super-cool guy with an affable personality. Wright is always willing to sign an autograph and pose for a photograph for one of his many fans. He is a real team player, including being the first to volunteer to dress up as Santa Claus for a holiday community event. But he also admits to being intensely competitive in nearly all areas of his life. "I'm ultra, ultra competitive," says the All-Star third baseman. "I guess it's growing up in a family of four boys. Whether it's Ping-Pong, or basketball in the backyard, or cards, I have to win." True to his word, Wright has already collected many prestigious baseball awards.

The serendipitous journey that led Wright to his position at third base for the New York Mets is just one of baseball's many great stories. While growing up in Virginia, Wright rooted for the Norfolk Tides, a Triple-A team near his hometown. "I got a kick out of going and seeing the Triple-A team play [in person] and then turning on the TV the next day or next week and seeing those same players I saw now on TV," says Wright. Meanwhile, Wright was completely unaware that he was watching his own future team. In 2001, Wright was selected in the first round of the baseball draft by the New York Mets, and he began his professional baseball career in their Minor League system. Before long, he moved up to the Mets' Triple-A team: the Norfolk Tides.

Through a combination of hard work, a competitive nature, and exceptional athleticism, Wright attracted loads of attention. While playing for the Tides and putting up great numbers, he got his Big League call-up on July 21, 2004. What was it like to run onto a Big

"If I get a couple of hits that day, I'll eat the same thing the next day. If I don't get any hits the day before, I will try to change it up and go with something else."

League field for the very first time and see his name on the JumboTron as the third base-man for the New York Mets? "It doesn't get much better than that," Wright says.

Yet, through it all, Wright maintains his regular-guy persona. When not playing pro-fessional baseball, he spends time in his downtown Manhattan home, and like many New Yorkers, he takes the subway to get around the city. Wright also spends time back in Vir-ginia visiting with his family and two dogs, appropriately named Homer and Shea. Wright is an avid fan of all sports and also enjoys listening to live music. "I love anything that has to do with sports," he says. "I go to a lot of sporting events in the winter—college basket-ball games, college football games, NBA, NFL games. I love playing fantasy football. I like to golf. All of my brothers play sports, so I like to root those guys on. I like hanging out and going to concerts."

When it comes to food, Wright has a few rituals as well as memorable meals from child-hood. Like his peers, Wright often eats the classic clubhouse food before a game—a peanut butter and jelly sandwich on whole wheat bread, or grilled chicken and rice, or black beans and rice. But for Wright this choice of pregame snack is directly linked to his performance the previous game day: "If I get a couple of hits that day, I'll eat the same thing the next day. If I don't get any hits the day before, I will try to change it up and go with something else."

When not in uniform, Wright enjoys food reminiscent of his mother's and grandmoth-er's Italian-American heritage. A salad of fresh tomato and mozzarella, known as a Cap-rese salad, remains a favorite. Like most kids, when told to eat his vegetables, especially green beans, he rebelled. Today, though, much to his surprise, his taste for green beans has changed and he eats them regularly. As for Wright's favorite on-the-go food, he's a pizza guy for sure: "I love, love, love pizza. I could eat pizza every day, and if I were going out to eat, I really like sushi." At the end of the day, however, Wright's favorite home-cooked meal will always be his grandmother's chicken Parmesan and tomato sauce, but without the side of pasta. "I'm not a big pasta guy," says Wright. And Wright's favorite dessert is all-American apple pie. This should come as no surprise, since baseball and apple pie have always gone hand in hand.

CHICKEN PARMESAN WITH FRESH TOMATO SAUCE

MAKES 6 SERVINGS

★ Chicken Parmesan is an all-time favorite not just for David Wright but for many of his teammates. Although Wright likes his chicken Parmesan plain without pasta, you can serve it with a side of spaghetti. This recipe has all the features of a top-notch Parm, with a light tomato and basil sauce and cheese-topped crunchy chicken.

Tomato Sauce

2 tablespoons olive oil

1 medium onion, finely chopped

2 garlic cloves, minced

1 28-ounce can crushed tomatoes

1 6-ounce can tomato sauce

⅓ cup finely chopped fresh basil

¼ teaspoon crushed red pepper flakes

Salt

Chicken

6 6-ounce skinless, boneless chicken breast halves

¾ teaspoon salt

½ teaspoon freshly ground black pepper

¾ cup all-purpose flour

3 large eggs

1¼ cups panko (Japanese bread crumbs)

¾ cup (3 ounces) freshly grated Parmesan, plus more for serving

2 tablespoons finely chopped fresh basil

1 tablespoon finely chopped fresh parsley

½ cup olive oil, plus more for the baking dish

8 ounces fresh mozzarella, thinly sliced

1 pound spaghetti, optional

1 To make the tomato sauce, heat the oil in a large saucepan over medium heat. Add the onion and cook, stirring occasionally, until tender, about 5 minutes. Add the garlic and cook until fragrant, about 1 minute. Add the crushed tomatoes, tomato sauce, ½ cup water, basil, and pepper flakes. Bring to a boil. Reduce the heat to medium-low and simmer, stirring occasionally, until slightly reduced, about 40 minutes. Season with salt. Remove from the heat and cover to keep warm.

2 Position a rack in the center of the oven and preheat to 400°F. Lightly oil a 15 x 10-inch baking dish. If making spaghetti, bring a large pot of lightly salted water to a boil over high heat.

3 Pound each chicken breast half between 2 heavy-duty plastic bags with a flat meat pounder to an even ½-inch thickness. Season the chicken with the salt and pepper. Spread the flour in a shallow dish. Beat the eggs in another shallow dish. Mix the panko, ¼ cup Parmesan, fresh basil, and parsley in a third shallow dish. Have a wax paper–lined baking sheet nearby.

4 One at a time, dip a chicken breast half in the flour, shaking off the excess flour. Dip in the eggs, letting the excess egg drip back into the bowl. Coat with the panko mixture and transfer to the baking sheet. Let stand for a few minutes to set the coating.

5 Heat the oil in a large skillet over medium-high heat. In batches, add the chicken and cook, turning once, until light golden brown on both sides, about 6 minutes. Using a slotted spatula, transfer to paper towels to drain briefly, then place in the baking dish.

6 Spoon the tomato sauce around the chicken. Top the chicken with the mozzarella and sprinkle with the remaining Parmesan. Bake until the cheese is melted and bubbling and the chicken is cooked through, 15–20 minutes.

7 Meanwhile, add the spaghetti, if you're making it, to the boiling water and cook, according to the package directions, until al dente. Drain well.

8 Divide the spaghetti, if using, evenly among 6 bowls. Top each with a chicken breast and sauce. Serve hot, with more Parmesan passed on the side. Transfer the chicken and sauce to plates and serve hot.

TOMATO, MOZZARELLA, AND GREEN BEAN SALAD

MAKES 4–6 SERVINGS

★ Cherry tomatoes and the thin French-style green beans make this Caprese salad a little classier than the typical version. If you can find it, use *mozzarella di bufala,* made from water buffalo milk, which is even creamier than regular fresh mozzarella.

8 ounces *haricots verts* or regular green beans, trimmed and cut into 1-inch lengths

2 tablespoons balsamic vinegar

¼ teaspoon salt

⅛ teaspoon freshly ground black pepper

½ cup extra-virgin olive oil

12 ounces cherry tomatoes, cut into halves

1 12-ounce ball fresh *mozzarella di bufala*, or regular fresh mozzarella, cut into bite-size pieces

2 tablespoons chopped fresh basil

1 Bring a large saucepan of lightly salted water to a boil over high heat. Add the green beans and cook until crisp-tender, about 3 minutes. Drain and rinse under cold running water. Drain again, and pat dry with paper towels.

2 Whisk the vinegar, salt, and pepper together in a medium bowl. Gradually whisk in the oil. Add the green beans and toss. Add the tomatoes and mozzarella, and toss again. Sprinkle with the basil and serve.

APPLE PIE

MAKES 8 SERVINGS

★ If you think that it would be hard to improve on the classic American apple pie, you might want to try this tweak: Apples have a huge variety of flavors (tart, sweet, honeylike) and textures (crisp, tender, crunchy), and mixing different apples makes for a more interesting pie.

1½ pounds sweet and firm apples, such as Golden Delicious or Empire or Fuji, peeled, cored, and cut into ¼-inch wedges

1½ pounds tart and crisp apples, such as Granny Smith or Cortland peeled, cored, and cut into ¼-inch wedges

½ cup sugar

½ cup packed light brown sugar

1 teaspoon ground cinnamon

¼ teaspoon freshly grated nutmeg

¼ teaspoon salt

2 tablespoons unsalted butter, cut into cubes

All-purpose flour, for rolling out the dough

Flaky Pie Dough (page 39)

1 Position a rack in the bottom third of the oven and preheat the oven to 400°F. Line a rimmed baking sheet with aluminum foil.

2 Combine the apples in a large bowl. You should have 7–8 cups. Add the granulated and brown sugars, cinnamon, nutmeg, and salt and mix well.

3 On a lightly floured work surface, roll out the larger pastry disk into a 13-inch-diameter round about ⅛ inch thick. Transfer to a 9-inch pie dish. Add the filling and scatter the butter on top. Roll out the remaining disk into a 10-inch-diameter round about ⅛ inch thick, and center on top of the filling. Cut out a 1-inch-diameter hole in the center of the top crust. Pinch the top and bottom crusts together and flute the edges. Place on the baking sheet.

4 Bake the pie for 15 minutes. Reduce the oven temperature to 350°F and continue baking until the crust is golden brown and the filling is bubbling in the center hole, about 1 hour. Transfer to a wire cake rack and let cool completely. Slice into wedges and serve.

METRIC CONVERSION TABLES

METRIC U.S. APPROXIMATE EQUIVALENTS

LIQUID INGREDIENTS

METRIC	U.S. MEASURES	METRIC	U.S. MEASURES
1.23 ML	¼ TSP.	29.57 ML	2 TBSP.
2.36 ML	½ TSP.	44.36 ML	3 TBSP.
3.70 ML	¾ TSP.	59.15 ML	¼ CUP
4.93 ML	1 TSP.	118.30 ML	½ CUP
6.16 ML	1¼ TSP.	236.59 ML	1 CUP
7.39 ML	1½ TSP.	473.18 ML	2 CUPS OR 1 PT.
8.63 ML	1¾ TSP.	709.77 ML	3 CUPS
9.86 ML	2 TSP.	946.36 ML	4 CUPS OR 1 QT.
14.79 ML	1 TBSP.	3.79 L	4 QTS. OR 1 GAL.

DRY INGREDIENTS

METRIC	U.S. MEASURES	METRIC	U.S. MEASURES
2 (1.8) G	1/16 OZ.	80 G	24/5 OZ.
3½ (3.5) G	1/8 OZ.	85 (84.9) G	3 OZ.
7 (7.1) G	¼ OZ.	100 G	3½ OZ.
15 (14.2) G	½ OZ.	115 (113.2) G	4 OZ.
21 (21.3) G	¾ OZ.	125 G	4½ OZ.
25 G	OZ.	150 G	5¼ OZ.
30 (28.3) G	1 OZ.	250 G	8 OZ.
50 G	1¾ OZ.	454 G	1 LB. 16 OZ.
60 (56.6) G	2 OZ.	500 G	1 LIVRE 173/5 OZ.

ACKNOWLEDGMENTS

I am deeply grateful to so many people who helped make this book come to life. It would never have been possible without the support of Major League Baseball. Specifically, I would like to thank Commissioner Bud Selig, Bob DuPuy, Rob Manfred, Tim Brosnan, Ethan Orlinsky, Bob Bowman, Tony Petitti, and Don Hintze. I am equally grateful to the Major League Baseball Players Association. I would like to express my sincere gratitude to Michael Weiner, Gene Orza, Judy Heater, Tom Slavin, Josh Orenstein, and Eric Rivera. They demonstrated immeasurable enthusiasm and commitment every step of the way.

A special thank you to team owners: Peter Angelos, Mark Attanasio, Bill DeWitt, Larry Dolan, Eddie Einhorn, Bill Giles, John Henry, Michael Illitch, Drayton McClane, Frank Mc-Court, Charles Monfort, David Montgomery, Jeff Moorad, Jim Pohlad, Jerry Reinsdorf, Hal Steinbrenner, Jennifer Steinbrenner Swindal, Stuart Sternberg, and Fred Wilpon. Thank you also to David Dombrowski, Randy Levine, and Jeff Wilpon.

Of course, a very special thank you is due to all the players who graciously agreed to participate and welcomed me into their kitchens: Lance Berkman, Miguel Cabrera, Andre Ethier, Adrian Gonzalez, Roy Halladay, Josh Hamilton, Ryan Howard, Derek Jeter, Josh Johnson, Paul Konerko, Evan Longoria, Joe Mauer, Dustin Pedroia, Albert Pujols, Hanley Ramirez, Alex Rodriguez, Johan Santana, Grady Sizemore, David Wright, and Chase Utley. Thank you also to Josh Beckett, Ryan Braun, Yunel Escobar, Ubaldo Jimenez, Nick Markakis, Chan Ho Park, and Ryan Zimmerman. I am equally grateful to the wives of the players, who were all so terrific, patient, and helpful: Cara Berkman, Rosangel Cabrera, Maggie Ethier, Betsey Gonzalez, Katie Hamilton, Heidi Johnson, Jennifer Konerko, Christina Markakis, Ri-Hye Park, Kelli Pedroia, Deidre Pujols, Elizabeth Ramirez, Yasmile Santana, and Jennifer Utley. And thank you to the moms of players: Donna Sizemore, Ellie Longoria, Teresa Mauer, and Bonnie Johnson.

I would also like to acknowledge the kindness of several agents who helped with player scheduling and more: specifically, Casey Close, Ned Bellelo, Jennifer Brasile, Seth Levinson, Andy Mota, Mike Moye, Billy Rose, and Joe Urban.

The support I received from the individual team clubs was extraordinary. I must first thank the Marlins for their endless hard work and dedication. Particularly, my heartfelt gratitude goes to David Samson, Larry Beinfest, Michael Hill, Dan Jennings, Bill Beck, Sean Cunningham, Spencer Linden, Beth McConville, Emmanuel Muñoz, and John Silverman. I'd like to extend a very special thanks to P. J. Loyello and Matt Roebuck for being tremendously helpful with overall communication, public relations, and seemingly endless details.

From other team clubs, the following individuals were amazingly accommodating and kind: Terry Francona (Boston Red Sox); Craig Landis, Scott Reifert, and Pat O'Connell

(Chicago White Sox); Jeff Sibel (Cleveland Indians); Brian Britten (Detroit Tigers); Mike Herman (Minnesota Twins); Brian Cashman, Joe Girardi, and Jason Zillo (New York Yankees); Rick Vaughn (Tampa Bay Rays); Stephen Grande (Houston Astros); Jason Carr (Chicago Cubs); Jay Albis (Colorado Rockies); Joe Torre and Joe Jareck (Los Angeles Dodgers); John Steinmiller (Milwaukee Brewers); Omar Minaya and Jay Horowitz (New York Mets); Charlie Manuel, Kevin Gregg, Greg Casterioto, and Bonnie Clark (Philadelphia Phillies); Tony LaRussa (St. Louis Cardinals); Brett Picciolo (San Diego Padres); and Mike Gazda (Washington Nationals).

A very personal thank you to Suzanne Grimes, Bill Hart, Wayne Katz, Alan Kahn, Susan Magrino, Bruce Rubin, Larry Shire, and Gay Talese for their professionalism, kindness, and enthusiasm.

A huge thank you to my agent, Susan Ginsburg, for her steadfast support and faith in me. Thank you also to the folks at Globe Pequot Press and Lyons Press for their hard work and invaluable guidance. My heartfelt thanks particularly to Janice Goldklang, Keith Wallman, Greg Hyman, Elizabeth Kingsbury, Inger Forland, and Bob Sembiante.

I am so appreciative of EJ Camp's stunning player photographs and tireless commitment and must thank Cathryn Collins for introducing us. A million thanks also to Ben Fink for his incredible food photography and the crew who helped out. And an enormous thank you to Alexandra Penney for her photography, invaluable advice, kindness, and friendship. My sincere gratitude to Rick Rodgers for his helpful recipe guidance, insight, and joie de vivre. And to Alison Lew and her Vertigo team, thank you for your graphic design brilliance.

Thank you to all the people who worked with me at various stages along the way, in the food and baseball worlds and beyond: Maribel Araujo, Rick Chavari, Myles Chefetz, David Corporan, Cesar Diaz, Constantine DeRosa, David Filliberti, Yvette Freixas, Lisa Gilson, Pat Hemm, Dean Hoffman, Bob Kanzler, Jeff Kavanaugh, Jason Oberle, Joe Ramaeker, Julia Soler, Oscar Vega, Vicky Vega, and Keli Zaloudek.

A heartfelt thank you for the encouragement of wonderful friends: Kit Bedrup, Mary Davidson, Max Davidson, Lori Jennings, Mindy Levine, Carol Levy, Larry Levy, Marie Martinez, Tino Martinez, Kathleen Reid, Vicki Rose, Carolyn Siskovic, Shelton Smith, Carolyn Sorkin, and Miho Umino.

A very special thank you to my supportive family, especially to Peggy Lavin, Patricia Roberts, and Susan Lavin Jones, for their sisterly advice and assurance.

And to my husband, Jeffrey, who makes baseball and food, and everything else in between, even more delicious.

RECIPE LIST

INDEX

ABOUT THE AUTHOR

A lifelong passion for food and baseball led Julie Loria to write her first book, *Diamond Dishes: From the Kitchens of Baseball's Biggest Stars.*

Throughout Julie's travels and career, food and baseball have been a constant. Her former career as a marketing and advertising executive in Boston gave way to watching baseball games and immersing herself in cooking courses in her spare time. A decade later, she left the corporate world and moved to Paris to pursue a career as an art dealer and to follow her culinary interests. With a newly acquired European acumen for fine art and food, Julie returned to the States, where she continues to be an avid baseball fan and food enthusiast.

Julie is the wife of Jeffrey Loria, owner of the Florida Marlins. They currently live in New York and Miami.